COLONIAL WILLIAMSBURG

Its Buildings and Gardens

COLONIAL WILLIAMSBURG

Its Buildings and Gardens

A DESCRIPTIVE TOUR OF THE RESTORED CAPITAL
OF THE BRITISH COLONY OF VIRGINIA

Revised Edition

BY

A. LAWRENCE KOCHER

AND

HOWARD DEARSTYNE

The COLONIAL WILLIAMSBURG FOUNDATION
Williamsburg, Virginia

Distributed by
HOLT, RINEHART AND WINSTON, INCORPORATED—NEW YORK

Distributed simultaneously in Canada by
Holt, Rinehart and Winston of Canada, Limited

Third printing, 1971

Revised edition copyright © 1961 by

THE COLONIAL WILLIAMSBURG FOUNDATION, WILLIAMSBURG, VIRGINIA

All rights reserved

First edition copyright © 1949

Library of Congress Catalogue Card Number: 61-11479

Colonial Williamsburg SBN: 910412-41-3
Holt, Rinehart & Winston SBN: 03-030735-X

Composition, printing, and binding by the Haddon Craftsmen, Scranton, Pennsylvania in Linotype Baskerville on paper supplied by the S. D. Warren Company, Boston, Massachusetts.

FOREWORD

THE VALUE of history lies in the perspective it gives us as we take up the problems of the present. Lawrence Kocher and Howard Dearstyne, by making us see here the intimate daily family life of eighteenth-century Williamsburg and the society of which it was a part, help us even more to see ourselves and our own time in sharper focus.

And insight, above everything else, is the purpose of Colonial Williamsburg —one-time capital of the great and powerful Virginia colony and the only capital of our colonial period which, after more than a century of sleep, could be awakened and reconstructed in its original form.

We hope that millions of Americans will find time and opportunity to visit Colonial Williamsburg in order that they may have the experience of stepping out of the present and losing themselves temporarily in the significant past. There is no better way for the modern American, man, woman, or child, to get a real emotional sense of the depth of his roots and the meaning of our nation's past.

Those who read this book—like those who come to Colonial Williamsburg— are urged to consider it only a foundation. The building of a free world can never be finished. We in our time must make our contribution. Colonial Williamsburg lives today to help all of us to feel strongly our heritage of liberty in order that we may build a better America and a better world in the twentieth century.

Colonial Williamsburg reminds us that the foundation of modern America is spiritual—a faith which began to take shape in Williamsburg and to be expressed there by some of the greatest of our forefathers. Nowhere else in colonial America was the democratic faith on which our nation has been built more eloquently expressed.

I think we cannot drink too deeply at this spring of our history. I think the authors in this book have helped you and me immeasurably to see the past so that we may understand and deal more effectively with the present.

KENNETH CHORLEY

President, Colonial Williamsburg
1935–1958

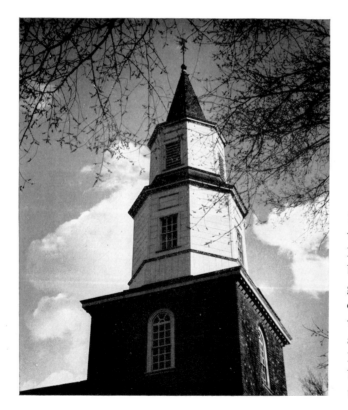

The steeple of Bruton Church was built in 1769 by Benjamin Powell of Williamsburg. Its bell, sometimes called Virginia's Liberty Bell, rang in celebration of the American victory at Saratoga in 1777 and pealed again six years later to proclaim the peace between Great Britain and the United States.

CONTENTS

FOREWORD   v

   I. *THE VIRGINIA PLANTERS' CAPITAL*   1

  II. *BUILDINGS AND BUILDERS OF WILLIAMSBURG*   11

 III. *THE MANNER OF FURNISHINGS*   25

 IV. *THE GARDENS OF WILLIAMSBURG*   35

  V. *THE RESTORATION OF AN AMERICAN TOWN*   43

 VI. *A PHOTOGRAPHIC TOUR OF WILLIAMSBURG*   51

     The Governor's Palace   52

     The George Wythe House   57

     The Brush-Everard House   60

     Bruton Parish Church   61

     The Magazine   62

     The Courthouse of 1770   63

     The Raleigh Tavern   64

     The Capitol   67

     The Public Gaol   70

     Houses   72

     Kitchens and Outbuildings   84

     Gates and Fences   86

     Arts and Crafts   88

     The College of William and Mary   92

     Merchants' Square   94

     The Information Center   96

     The Abby Aldrich Rockefeller Folk Art Collection   97

 VII. *BIBLIOGRAPHICAL NOTES*   98

VIII. *INDEX*   100

 IX. *CREDITS FOR ILLUSTRATIONS*   104

The Virginia Planters' Capital

*"The moral influence of the large plantation
. . . fostered habits of self-reliance in individual
men; it assisted in promoting an intense love
of liberty; it strengthened the ties of family and
kinship at the very time that it cultivated the
spirit of general hospitality."—Bruce*

WHEN THE FIRST settlers of Virginia landed at Jamestown, they found themselves in a most unfriendly environment; they were confronted by a mysterious wilderness, unfamiliar flora and fauna, and a strange and hostile race of men. In their struggle for survival in this New World, these early colonists had little opportunity to develop architecture of lasting significance. There was, however, the immediate need for shelter and protection. Carpenters and bricklayers were put to work, and houses soon sprang up within a wooden stockade. These first shelters were roughhewn; one seventeenth-century writer considered them as devoid of architectural beauty as a barn, lacking both chimneys and partitions. Still later, even homes of prominent planters were often described as "simple and plain."

On the other hand, structures of considerable architectural pretension were soon planned along the James and York rivers. In Surry County, for example, the country seat known as Bacon's Castle was under construction within a half century of the landing at Jamestown. This Jacobean building, although small compared with English mansions, has an elaboration of detail in its doorways, mantels, and clustered chimneys that can be associated only with the "designed" house. Similar architectural ambitions were evident in churches such as St. Luke's near Smithfield, the church at Jamestown, and the early buttressed church at Middle Plantation. And, within one hundred years of Jamestown's founding, the notable public buildings of Williamsburg—the Wren Building at the College of William and Mary, the Capitol, and the Governor's Palace—were either built or under construction.

PLANTATION SOCIETY

In colonial Virginia, architecture was developed to meet the requirements and tastes of a plantation society, a society in which social prestige and political power depended primarily on tobacco, "the Indian weed" which John Rolfe improved by crossbreeding. After the land was safe from Indian attack, and the woodlands sufficiently cleared, the broad fertile Tidewater was dotted with plantations, large and small, with their mansions and outbuildings. The broad-leafed plant sustained a planter aristocracy which prided itself on its great estates, such as Westover, Berkeley, Carter's Grove, Tuckahoe, Brandon, Stratford, and Shirley.

Except for certain manufactured articles, which were imported from England, the planter became largely self-sufficient. The wealthy planter was master of a small village. The plantation house, with its numerous dependent buildings, was an expression of this remarkable community. At an appropriate distance from the mansion were the kitchen, smokehouse, dairy, storehouse, washhouse, coach house, and stable. There might even be a schoolhouse. Near the tobacco fields were the rude slave quarters. Timber for building was cut from the planter's own land and sawed at his own mill. Brick used in his mansion was molded, and burned in a kiln, from clay dug

Loading tobacco ships on the James. Tobacco "was largely instrumental in moulding the social classes and political structure of the Colony. . . . It even exerted a powerful influence upon religion and morals."—Wertenbaker.

on his own plantation. Hogsheads in which tobacco was shipped were made in his cooper's shop. Shoes were fashioned in his own shoemaker's shop, out of leather provided by his tannery. At the smithy, the plantation's blacksmiths hammered out hardware, shod horses, and repaired farm implements and wagons.

The plantation house was patterned after English mansions, but was adapted to meet the needs of plantation life. Spacious, high-ceilinged rooms offered comfort in summer heat and were well suited for entertainment; for, if plantation life imposed its burden of cares, it also had its amenities. There was a constant interchange of visits among the plantations, which were rarely without guests. Philip Fithian, in 1773 tutor at Nomini Hall, the Westmoreland County home of Councilor Robert Carter, makes numerous references to balls, barbecues, billiards, card games, and other social events. Children of the planters acquired social graces early, and were usually given dancing lessons; Fithian, observing one lesson conducted by an exacting tutor, noted in his diary: "There were several Minuets danced with great ease and propriety; after which the whole company Joined in country-dances, and it was indeed beautiful to admiration, to see such a number of young persons, set off by dress to the best Advantage, moving easily, to the sound of well performed Music."

WILLIAMSBURG AS CAPITAL

Williamsburg itself was the political and social metropolis of this plantation gentry, and reflects this role in its architectural development. Because of the predominantly agricultural character of the colony, Williamsburg, unlike such populous trading marts as Boston, New York, or Philadelphia, resembled "a good Country Town in England"; its population (white and Negro included) never exceeded two thousand. Yet it served as the seat of government and as the cultural center for one of Britain's largest and most powerful colonies; its size belies its importance in shaping the American past. Its political significance is intimated in the Capitol; its prestige for the Crown in the Governor's Palace; its cultural role in Bruton Church and the Wren Building of the College of William and Mary.

The historical and architectural significance of Williamsburg is largely confined to its tenure as capital of Virginia, during the years 1699 to 1780. The town was settled as Middle Plantation in 1633, as an outpost against Indian attack. In 1699, the capital was removed from Jamestown to this site, and the town was renamed Williamsburg, in honor of King William III. In 1780, during a critical stage of the Revolutionary War, the capital was moved to Richmond, which was considered "more safe and central than any other town situated on navigable water." Its mission fulfilled, Williamsburg fell into a decline. Its historic importance was to lie buried for a century and a half.

Despite the care with which colonial Williamsburg has been recreated, it is often difficult for the modern-day visitor to visualize the

town exactly as it was in the eighteenth century. To know its buildings and gardens it is also necessary to understand something of its political masters, merchants and craftsmen, and cultural and religious leaders. Without this understanding, the city as restored today is no more than a museum piece. Williamsburg in the past was a living town, and it is only through constant awareness of those who made it famous that the significance of eighteenth-century Virginia and its small but important capital can be appreciated.

"PUBLICK TIMES"

For most of the year, Williamsburg was a small college town and market place, but twice annually, during "publick times," the planters' capital sprang to life. It was then that the legislature usually met, and the courts were in session. A crowded social and political calendar attracted men of every pocketbook and profession from all parts of the colony. The population of the town doubled almost overnight, and every available inn, tavern, and private house was packed to overflowing.

The most prominent persons of the colony came to Williamsburg at these times and often brought their families for the entertainments which were planned for the season. There were elegant dinners

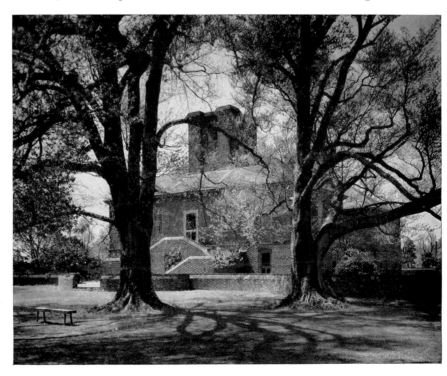

Stratford, a plantation house little changed since it was built, 1725-30. Here was born one of Virginia's most famous sons, Robert E. Lee.

and balls at the Governor's Palace for officials and their wives, and at the taverns hosts and dancing masters offered assembly balls and suppers to all who cared to purchase tickets. Traveling theatrical troupes planned their best dramatic performances to coincide with public times and adjusted admission charges to attract all classes to seats in the boxes, the pit, or the gallery. Horse races, too, enlivened the scene with crowds of spectators closely packed along the sides of the track, enjoying their favorite sport.

Both to stimulate trade and to amuse the crowds, Williamsburg's fairs were scheduled to run for three days each spring and fall. A notice appearing in a *Virginia Gazette* of 1739 reveals their nature and objectives:

WHEREAS TWO FAIRS are appointed to be held in this City . . . out of a laudable Design to encourage the Trade thereof, and to be a Means of promoting a general Commerce or Traffick among Persons that want to buy or sell, either the Product or Manufactures of the Country. . . .

IT *is therefore Agreed upon, and Ordered,* That the following . . . shall be given as *Bounties.* . . .

To the Person that brings most Horses to the said FAIR, and there offers them to Publick Sale . . . a Pistole. . . .

To the Person that brings most Cows, Steers, or other horned Cattle . . . a Pistole shall be given. . . .

AND for the *Entertainment* and *Diversion* of all Gentlemen and others, that shall resort thereto, the following PRIZES are given to be contended for . . . *viz.*

A good Hat to be Cudgell'd for. . . .

A Saddle of 40 *s.* Value, to be run for, once round the Mile Course, adjacent to this City. . . .

A Pair of Silver Buckles, Value 20 *s.* to be run for by Men, from the *College* to the *Capitol.* . . .

A Pair of Pumps to be danc'd for by Men.

A handsome Firelock to be exercis'd for. . . .

A Pig, with his Tail soap'd, to be run after. . . .

Fashionable head-dresses of 1780

TRADES AND CRAFTS

Williamsburg was not a large trading center, but its shopkeepers and craftsmen made the most of pub-

lic times to display the finest goods produced in the colony and articles "after the newest fashion" imported from England. The latest creations in clothing and household furnishings often appeared in Williamsburg sooner than in out-of-the-way towns in England; planters had the latest London modes to choose from, and the shops did a thriving business.

Although never an important manufacturing city, Williamsburg at one time or another during the colonial period did produce furniture, candles,

JAMES GEDDY,
GOLDSMITH,
NEAR THE CHURCH, WILLIAMSBURG,

HAS just imported from *London* a genteel assortment of PLATE and JEWELLERY; he has likewise on hand all sorts of country made GOLD and SILVER WORK, which he will sell at lower rates than usual.----Old SILVER taken in exchange for new work, at 7s. per ounce, and GOLD at 5l. 5s.----He repairs his own work, that fails in a reasonable time, without any expence to the purchaser. 4

coaches, saddles and harness, jewelry, shoes, hosiery, and wigs. For the most part, these articles were purchased by townspeople. In its early days, particularly, Williamsburg was almost completely dependent on England for manufactured articles; the extent of this dependence, even as late as 1752, is suggested by a notice in the *Virginia Gazette* announcing the arrival of "A FRESH Cargoe of live human Hairs, all ready curl'd and well prepared by the best Hands in *London.*" With the passage of the Stamp Act and other restrictive measures, however, relations with England became more and more strained, imports declined, and home crafts and manufactures received increasing support and encouragement.

Typical of the response to such measures is a notice which appeared in the *Gazette* in 1769 requesting ladies and gentlemen to turn in their old gold and silver to James Geddy, goldsmith, "[who], as he has not imported any jewellery this season . . . flatters himself he will meet with encouragement." A Committee for the Encouragement of Arts and Manufactures offered prizes in 1765 to persons producing the most well-dressed hemp. At Capitol Landing, a mile from town, a factory was established which announced that it was prepared to turn out cloth as good as could be woven in England. The introduction of the mulberry

Opposite, **Barber and Wigmaker's Shop.**

tree to Virginia in the hope of establishing a silk industry did not meet with the success expected, although a notice in the *Gazette* in 1775 reported that a certain Mr. Estave collected enough cocoons in a single year to produce one hundred pounds of silk fit for manufacture.

No discussion of trades and crafts in Williamsburg would be complete which failed to mention William Parks and printing. Parks opened an office on Duke of Gloucester Street about 1730 and printed and sold many books, including William Stith's *The History*

TYPOGRAPHIA.

AN

O D E,

ON

PRINTING.

Infcrib'd to the Honourable

WILLIAM GOOCH, *Efq;*

His Majefty's Lieutenant-Governor, and Commander in Chief of the Colony of *VIRGINIA*.

----------- *Pleni funt omnes Libri, plenæ fapientum voces, plena Exemplorum vetuftas ; quæ jacerent in Tenebris omnia, nifi Literarum Lumen accederet.*

Cic. Orat. pro Archia.

WILLIAMSBURG:
Printed by W**ILLIAM** P**ARKS.** M,DCC,XXX.

One of the first examples of printing in Virginia was published in 1730 by William Parks, founder of the *Virginia Gazette*. It was the earliest American appreciation of the press and was "occasion'd by the setting up a printing-press in Williamsburg."

of the First Discovery and Settlement of Virginia, The Whole Body of the Laws of Virginia, The Poor Planter's Physician, Poems by a Gentleman of Virginia, and numerous other publications concerning religion, music, school subjects, and military tactics. Through his office and those of his successors, books and current London magazines were imported and sold. The first number of the *Virginia Gazette,* oldest newspaper in the colony, was issued by Parks in 1736. Thirteen years later, with the aid of Benjamin Franklin, Parks established a paper mill on the outskirts of Williamsburg, advertising that he desired "all Persons to save their old *Linen Rags,* for making Paper," adding that "As this is the first Mill of the Kind, that ever was erected in this Colony, and has cost a very considerable Sum of Money," he hoped "to meet with Encouragement suitable to so useful an Undertaking." Parks, who was a fine typographer and a skillful editor, has justly been called a dean among early American printers, and his influence on the culture of the city and colony was extensive.

CULTURE AND RELIGION

The presence in the town of the College of William and Mary, founded in 1693 and, after Harvard, the oldest college in the colonies, helped make Williamsburg the cultural center of Virginia. The relationship between the College and the colonial government was close; William and Mary was actually represented in the House of Burgesses, the only college in the colonies enjoying such a privilege. Students included Thomas Jefferson, Benjamin Harrison, James Monroe, John Tyler, John Marshall, Edmund Randolph, and others influential in America's formative years. Among distinguished faculty members was George Wythe, tutor of Jefferson and founder of the first course in law at an American college.

The site of the College was ideal. The act of 1699, directing the development of Williamsburg, had reflected that "it will prove highly advantageous and beneficiall to his Majesty's Royall Colledge of William & Mary to have the conveniences of a towne near the same." Located in the center of the social, cultural, and political life of the colony, the College could offer students first-hand study of colonial society and government. Perhaps the largest debt owed to one man by the young College was due the Reverend James Blair, energetic and fiery Scottish clergyman

Household utensils in the Palace Kitchen. We note with admiration the grace and endurance of such homely objects as ladles, draining and skimming spoons, long-handled fireplace forks, molds, and skewers.

who fought hard for its inception and became its first president. A notice in the London *Post Boy* in 1706 shows the rapidly growing reputation of the College: "Some . . . from Virginia tell us that the College which had been lately founded there . . . is so crowded with Students, that they begin to think of enlarging the College, for it seems divers from Pensilvania, Maryland, and Carolina send their Sons thither to be educated."

Virginia was fortunate in having a number of royal governors who were men of learning and who supported and encouraged the work of the College and the cultural life of Williamsburg. Among these were Governor Fauquier, greatly admired by Thomas Jefferson, and Lord Botetourt, in whose honor the Botetourt medals for scholarship have been awarded by the College continuously since that time. Even Governor Dunmore, later the object of the colonists' suspicion and hatred, was a sponsor of the Society for the Advancement of Useful Knowledge (1773), through which the founders hoped "to direct the Attention of their Countrymen to the Study of Nature, with a View of multiplying the Advantages that may result from this Source of Improvement. . . . It is therefore the Intention of this Society to rescue from Oblivion every useful Essay."

Eighteenth-century Virginians loved and appreciated music; planters' children were expected to learn to sing or play some instrument. Many music teachers gave lessons in the town and toured the plantations to instruct in the violin, harpsichord, and pianoforte. Outstanding among these was Cuthbert Ogle, whose inventory of effects lists a fine collection of sonatas and concertos by English composers and many books of Handel's songs and oratorios. Psalmody was a part of services at Bruton Church. Fiddling contests were events at every fair, and home concerts were frequent. Jefferson joined with Governor Fauquier and others in impromptu chamber musicales at the Palace. Theater patrons were often entertained between acts by performers on French horns, trumpets, and other instruments.

"The [Wren] Building is beautiful and commodious, being first modelled by Sir Christopher Wren, adapted to the Nature of the Country by the Gentlemen there. . . ."—Hugh Jones, 1724.

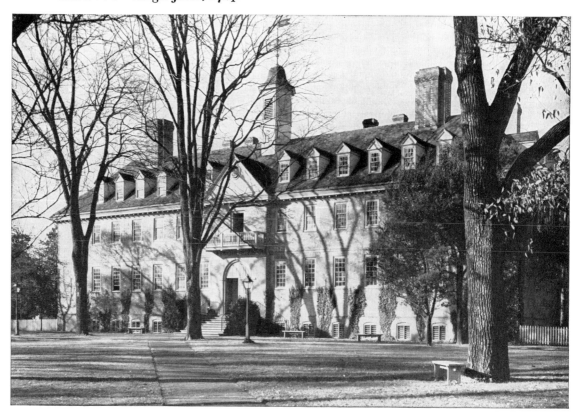

Between 1716 and 1718 William Levingston erected the first theater in America on the east side of the Palace Green, proposing to present in this "good Substantial house commodious for Acting" comedies, "drolls," and other kinds of stage plays. Many of the productions were amateur. The *Virginia Gazette*, for example, announced in 1736 the performance there of *The Tragedy of Cato* by the "young Gentlemen of the College" and other plays by the "Gentlemen and Ladies of this Country."

Although this pioneer venture at first met with hearty approval, and the playhouse was filled night after night, it was forced to close two decades later for financial reasons. A second playhouse was erected in 1751 near the Capitol. Here Lewis Hallam and his company from London made their American debut in *The Merchant of Venice*. Hallam announced that he had brought with him "Scenes, Cloaths and Decorations . . . all entirely new, extremely rich . . . excell'd by none in Beauty and Elegance, so that the Ladies and Gentlemen may depend on being enter-

Pulpit of Bruton Church. According to an early writer, Bruton was "adorned as the best Churches in London."

tain'd in as polite a Manner as at the Theatres in *London*." Patrons of Hallam's theater included many prominent colonists. George Washington was an enthusiastic playgoer, noting in his diary that he

The Reverend Mr. George Whitefield, impetuous Anglican priest who with the Wesleys began the Methodist movement, "arrived in December, 1739, at Williamsburg, and preached there in Bruton Church, producing great excitement." Portrait by John Wollaston.

"Dined at the President's and went to the Play" or that he "Reach'd Williamsburg before Dinner, and went to the Play in the Afternoon."

Doubtless one of the factors influencing the choice of Middle Plantation as the seat of government in Virginia was the presence there of Bruton Church. This church, a Gothic structure with buttresses, which had been completed in 1683, was not adequate to serve as court church of the colony; and so a new church, the same building which stands today, was erected between 1711 and 1715 from plans furnished by Governor Spotswood, and became the center of religious life in the new capital. Here the governors came each Sunday to worship, as did the members of the Council and the House of Burgesses when in Williamsburg. The aristocracy of Williamsburg and near-by plantations assembled here to listen to the sermons and to display their best attire. The students of the College occupied a special gallery reserved for them.

The people of Williamsburg and the surrounding country sought spiritual guidance at Bruton Church

By Permission of the Honble *ROBERT DINWIDDIE*, Efq; His Majefty's Lieutenant-Governor, and Commander in Chief of the Colony and Dominion of *Virginia*.

By a Company of Comedians, from LONDON, At the Theatre in Williamsburg, On *Friday* next, being the 15th of *September*, will be prefented, A PLAY, Call'd, THE

MERCHANT of *VENICE*.

(Written by *Shakefpear*.)

in times of stress, as when periods of drought or epidemics of "distemper" visited the colony, or when the political situation became critical. In 1774, for example, when Parliament ordered the sealing of the Port of Boston, the House of Burgesses set aside June 1 as a day of fasting, humiliation, and prayer. On this day, the members of the House proceeded to the church in a body "to implore the divine interposition, for averting the heavy Calamity which threatens destruction to our Civil Rights, and the Evils of civil

War." Washington wrote in his diary that he "Went to [Bruton] Church and fasted all day."

Life in eighteenth-century Williamsburg followed closely the cultural patterns of the mother country. Under the influence of new forces at work in a new land, however, colonial Virginians moved steadily toward new patterns; they became less English and more distinctly citizens of Virginia and of the new nation in the making. It was the life and customs of the country which dictated the manner of its architecture. Although this architecture was based originally on the mode of building already established in eighteenth-century England, it was "adapted to the Nature of the Country" by the local builders and craftsmen and became definitely Virginian. It changed as life in the colony changed and varied from place to place under the influence of local conditions; thus Williamsburg, too, developed an architecture of its own. The architects of the restoration sought to recapture this local individuality in rebuilding the town; in their own words, "[it was] the essence of restoration philosophy so to comprehend the eighteenth century in England and so to study its variations in the Colonies, especially Virginia, that the Georgian mode and manner were eventually translated into a vernacular *specifically of Williamsburg*."

Buildings and Builders of Williamsburg

*"Williamsburg, at the Revolution, was a town
of beauty and of architectural significance; its
major buildings were milestones in the history
of American style, its Palace Garden perhaps
the most beautiful in America."*
—*Fiske Kimball*

IN THE YEAR 1759 the traveler Andrew Burnaby graphically described Williamsburg as a place for "agreeable residence." He observed that the town was "regularly laid out in parallel streets, intersected by others at right angles; [it] has a handsome square in the center, through which runs the principal street, one of the most spacious in North-America. . . . At the ends of this street are two public buildings, the college and the capitol, and . . . the whole makes a handsome appearance." This "handsome appearance" owed much to careful town planning, in which principles still in use today were followed. The site selected was an eminence between two rivers in a region reasonably free from the pestilential dampness which had made Jamestown so unhealthful.

THE TOWN PLAN

The character of the new town at Middle Plantation was established in a plan provided in 1699 by Governor Francis Nicholson, who soon afterwards was to boast of being "the Founder of a new City.'" He laid out the streets and open squares and located the proposed public buildings. What proved to be his most notable achievement was the stipulation that each house lot should be one-half acre in size. It was furthermore Nicholson's view that each person should have his own dwelling place, with a sufficient quantity of ground for his house, his garden, and orchard. The act directing the building of Williamsburg, a measure of importance in the history of modern town planning, specified "that two hundred & twenty Acres . . . be . . . sett a part for ground on which the said City shall be built and erected according to the form

and manner laid downe in the said draught or plott."

Analysis of the plan itself underscores the significance of this document. The plot for each home builder was precisely specified; comments were even made on the design of the houses, and their set-back from the street was determined. In several respects the regulations read like a zoning ordinance of a twentieth-century suburban community:

"The Said City of Williamsburgh shall be laid out and proportioned into halfe Acres every of Which halfe Acre shall be a distinct lott of ground to be built upon in manner and forme as is hereafter expressed that is to say that whosoever shall build in the maine Street of the said City of Williamsburgh as laid out in the aforesaid draught or Plott shall not build a house less then tenn foot pitch [meaning from ground floor to the second floor] and the front of each house shall come within Six foot of the street and not nearer and that the houses in the Severall lots in the Said main street shall front a like."

These regulations were made in 1699, when other cities in the American colonies were also being planned—Charleston, for example, in 1672, and Philadelphia in 1682, though neither had a plan conceived in so comprehensive or so grand a manner.

This was a time of new ideas in town planning. In the proposed layout for Williamsburg, several novel principles were incorporated that may well have been suggested by the schemes for the rebuilding of London following the Great Fire of 1666. In the plan of Williamsburg, as proposed by Governor Nicholson, Duke of Gloucester Street was made a wide esplanade, skillfully terminated by the Capitol at one end and by

The St. George Tucker House Kitchen, distinguished by its massive chimney.

the College at the other. Comparing this for a moment with the unrealized plan for the rebuilding of London prepared by Sir Christopher Wren, the observer will note similar vistas that end with churches and public buildings. Similarities in the width of streets were also marked. Duke of Gloucester Street was to be six poles, or ninety-nine feet, in width. Wren had called for ninety feet as the proposed width of the three principal streets of London. In the plan of John Evelyn, a farsighted English amateur architect who had hoped to rebuild London on a more orderly and spacious scale, the width of the main avenues had been specified as one hundred feet.

The College is at one end of Duke of Gloucester Street, the Capitol at the other. At a right angle to this street is Palace Green, terminated by the Palace.

The Williamsburg scheme is climaxed by placing the Governor's Palace as a terminus facing a long and wide grassy plot. This approach to the Palace is given additional incisiveness and interest by flanking the grassy area with catalpas.

THE WILLIAMSBURG HOUSE

The half-acre plot specified for each Williamsburg house was the formula that gave an entirely new aspect to the settlement on the peninsula. Free-standing houses were built, with a garden and orchard space. The spacious lots were soon dotted with outbuildings, all having a design related to the main house and to the gardens. This was decidedly unlike the cramped quarters of the narrow and medieval row-housing at Jamestown. Whereas the size of Jamestown was restricted by its peninsula site, Governor Nicholson's new town could spread out toward either the York River or the James.

One type of house which in time came to be charac-

teristic of Williamsburg was a story and a half in height with a steep shingled roof, suggesting to one

Bracken House. Early form of house plan, "one room deep," having a projecting chimney at each end. In some instances there was no central hallway, but stairs were within one of the rooms.

observer the appearance of "an inverted ship with ridged hull in the air." This house usually had a great chimney of brick at one or both ends, and its windows, placed on each side of a doorway, were often spaced with Vitruvian regularity. Dormers gave life to the roof.

Hugh Jones, in *The Present State of Virginia*, describes Williamsburg as it appeared in the years 1721 through 1724. "Here," he says, "as in other

Bracken House. A typical Williamsburg house, one story and a half in height, having a steep roof in the form of an A.

Parts, they build with Brick, but most commonly with Timber lined with Cieling, and cased with feather-edged Plank, painted with white Lead and Oil, covered with Shingles of *Cedar*, &c. tarr'd over at first; with a Passage generally through the Middle of the House for an Air-Draught in Summer." Governor Berkeley's house at Green Spring, two miles from Jamestown, was, according to the historian Bruce, described by a contemporary as having a "wide hall characteristic of all the larger dwellings in Virginia at this time. . . . The wideness of the hall was for the purpose of obtaining the fullest ventilation, the climate of this part of the Colony in the warm season being oppressive and unwholesome."

The house types of Williamsburg are in some respects local or indigenous to Virginia. All are moderate in size, yet comfortable and commodious. Their architecture is of a practical sort, without ornament or pretense, and their exteriors are mostly free from columns or other evidences of "the orders of architecture." With the single exception of the Governor's Palace, none of them recalls the academic grandeur of plantation mansions such as Westover, Shirley, or Rosewell. It is this simple type of house to which Isaac Ware refers in his *Complete Body of Architecture* (1756), and which, he says, appeals to the man in the country, who may be desirous of building "without columns, or other expensive decorations."

Although altered somewhat from decade to decade,

"Two-room-deep" plan with side hallway (Tayloe House).

three general plan types of Williamsburg houses of the eighteenth century may be identified and described. The first may be called the "one-room-deep" plan. This has a hallway at its center and a room at either side. Tidewater Virginia had many such houses,

Gambrel roof with steep lower slope (Tayloe House), devised so as to obtain greater floor area within the roof.

a type rarely found in New England. This room arrangement apparently grew out of the seventeenth-century dwelling, "built of wood, yet contrived so delightfull, that your ordinary houses in England are not so handsome." The plan illustration of the Bracken House reproduced on the previous page shows the rooms flanking the hallway to be of unequal width. The number of windows on either side of the doorway sometimes varies. This type of house had a chimney, usually an outside chimney, at one or both ends of the building.

A second type became popular near the middle of the eighteenth century; this was the "two-room-deep" plan, with a side hall. This one-sided plan appears, from its several examples, to have been a favorite arrangement. The Orrell, Tayloe, and Lightfoot houses are typical. The front room, often designated "the parlor," was usually almost square and had a corner fireplace as did also the back room. The chimney was contained within the wall and one stack of flues served the two rooms. The corner fireplace was an innovation of the time of William and Mary.

John Evelyn speaks of it disdainfully in 1692, saying that "This plan of placing fireplaces in the corner

WYTHE

The Wythe House. Third plan type, two rooms deep with center hall.

of rooms has come into fashion . . . I predict that it will spoil many noble houses and rooms if followed. It does only well in very small and trifling rooms." It was, however, economical to construct, and the added

heat reflected into the room because of the angle of the walls made it efficient. Finally, as one writer says, "it offers a more prominent position for a painting"!

A third and much more pretentious type of Williamsburg house was also two rooms in depth, but with a center hall and chimneys built within the area of the plan. The Governor's Palace is based on this arrangement, as are also the George Wythe, Robert Carter, and Allen-Byrd plans, and that of the President's House at the College. Most houses of this type have four rooms on each floor. The Robert Carter House is exceptional in having, with its one stairway, a second hall at the corner.

MATERIALS

For the small house, wood framing faced with weatherboarding continued to be the common construction method in the Virginia colony throughout the eighteenth century. The popularity of wood is ascribed to a contemporary prejudice that houses

The front portion of The Quarter, 16 feet deep by 24 feet wide, suggests the original form of some early Williamsburg houses. This basic dimension may still be seen in many outbuildings.

Thomas Mott Shaw

Brickmaking in Williamsburg in the colonial manner: mixing the clay by mule power and a workman filling the brick molds.

Old colonial brickwork of the Public Records Office, showing texture of brick and glazed headers.

with brick walls were damp and consequently less wholesome. Jefferson, writing of construction in Virginia in 1784, notes that "private buildings are very rarely constructed of brick or stone; much the greater portion being of scantling and boards, plastered with lime." Williamsburg, however, had its fair share of brick buildings, showing usually a traditional use of English bond below the water table and Flemish bond above. English bond can readily be recognized by the surface pattern made up of a row of "header" bricks placed over a row of "stretchers." Flemish bond has alternating headers and stretchers over the entire wall surface. Madame Knight, a noted traveler of the period, remarked on the appearance of Flemish bond in New York: "Bricks in some of the houses are of divers colors and laid in checkers." Diamond patterns sometimes supplement the checkers on the eastern shore of Virginia and in Princess Anne County. One authority, writing in the early part of the nineteenth century, thus appraised the two methods: "Flemish bond is deemed the neatest and most beautiful, but is attended with a great deal of inconvenience in the execution, and in most cases does not unite the parts of a wall with the same degree of firmness as the English bond."

Bricks used for buildings of the town were burned on or near the site and were laid in a coarse oyster-shell lime mortar. The gray-green glaze seen on some headers was imparted by burning the bricks in a kiln fired with oakwood. Only those bricks nearest the heat acquired the glazed surface. The use of bricks rubbed down to a smooth surface or to a molded profile was a favorite means of imparting finish to a building. The rubbing was done with sharp sand on a piece of millstone or by rubbing two bricks together. Most of the colonial brick buildings in Williamsburg have rubbed brick for arches, water tables, and string-courses, and at the corners of their walls and chimneys. The finest example of original rubbed moldings is that in the pediment edge of the entrance doorway of the Public Records Office, near the Capitol. The versatility of the artisans who produced these and the moldings of the chimney tops is one of the most striking achievements of this age of craftsmanship.

The controversial theory that brick sizes can be used to determine the age of a building receives little support in Williamsburg, where a wide variety of sizes occurs. Bricks of largest dimensions appear in

Public Records Building, **office of the Secretary of the Colony. The doorway design with its molded brick pediment and projecting brick pilasters was used repeatedly in Tidewater Virginia and closely resembles that of near-by Carter's Grove.**

brick walls and pavements. The statute bricks of England, by act of Parliament, 1776, were 2½ by 4 by 9 inches; this can be compared with an earlier statute brick of 1685, 2¼ by 4¼ by 8¾ inches. These British statute sizes did have their echo in the Virginia colony, however. The bricks for a wall around St. Peter's Church, New Kent County, were in 1719 specified to be "according to the Statute something Less then Nine Inches in Length, two Inches and one quarter thick, and four Inches and one quarter Wide."

Numerous studies of masonry building in America before the Revolution report that brick was brought from England as ballast. It has become customary to refute this claim. Certainly, most building sites in town and on plantations were the scene of brick burning, and clay suitable for brick was found everywhere in Tidewater Virginia. There does exist, however, a reasonable basis for the claim that brick

occasionally was imported into the Virginia colony. This importation as ballast is implied by an act of October, 1748, "That nothing herein contained shall be construed to prohibit or restrain the master of any ship or other vessel, bringing limestone, chalk, bricks, or stone for building, to lade or put the same on board any other vessel, in order to be carried or transported to any place he shall think fit."

Outside wood walls of dwellings and dairy buildings were sometimes filled with partly burned bricks. This construction was vastly superior as insulation and also more fireproof than ordinary lathing and plastering on wood frame. The outer walls of the John Blair House and a few others were found to be of this type. A recommendation was made in the colonies that, "Partitions [of wood] between rooms . . . might be superseded, for greater security, by partitions of 4 inch brick walls, vulgarly called 'bricknogging'.

17

. . . Many houses have been burned by servants sticking candles against wooden partitions."

THE VIRGINIA CHIMNEY

The huge outside house chimneys so familiar in the Williamsburg landscape appear to be typical of Tidewater Virginia, although not restricted to the colony. They derive from earlier examples in England and are associated there with the seventeenth century. Following the Great Fire of 1666, chimney stacks for London were regulated "within the wall face."

The characteristic Virginia chimney is of brick, broad at the base so as to give a roomy fireplace within, sloping at the sides to a smaller upper shaft. Because of the need to make domestic fires safe, the chimney top rises past the gable of the house without coming into contact with shingles or other woodwork. This chimney form may have followed closely that of the original wood-framed or "catted" chimney. The wooden prototypes appear to have been common in early days. Samuel Groome in 1683 wrote one of the Proprietors in London that his chimney was "made with timber and clay as the manner of this country is to build." Examples of wood-frame chimneys continued to be built for occasional outbuildings in Virginia until the end of the nineteenth century.

Outside brick chimney of the Todd House near Fredericksburg. The sloping flanks indicate the position of the fireplaces within.

WILLIAMSBURG INFLUENCE

Paralleling the political and social prestige of Williamsburg, its architecture too had a wide influence. As early as 1665, long before the town was established, a church was ordered built in Middlesex County "according to the Modall of the Middle-plantacoñ Church in all Respects." Later, in 1719, when an enclosing wall and gates were voted for St. Peter's Church in New Kent County, the instructions to the builder were for "Handsom Gates made after the fform of Iron Gates . . . with a hollow Spire a Top. . . . [The] Wall to be in all Respects as well Done as the Capitol wall in Williams: Burgh." The town of Hanover Court House at mid-century specified that its new powder magazine follow in design the Magazine at Williamsburg. It is known also that builders living in Williamsburg—Morris, Cary, Minetree, and others—were commissioned to construct plantation houses in the surrounding country.

"Catted" chimney of Virginia cabin. The "cats" were pieces of "straw and clay worked together in pretty large rolls and laid between the wooden posts."

Opposite, **chimney of the James Anderson Kitchen. The broad base of kitchen chimneys in Williamsburg sometimes enclosed an oven as well as a fireplace.**

BUILDING THE CAPITOL AND PALACE

An act of June 7, 1699, directed the building of the Capitol in Williamsburg. This structure is a notable landmark in colonial American architecture, partly because it is one of the first public buildings of size erected in the colonies, and partly because it gave the first evidence of transition from the essential medievalism of Bacon's Castle to what was to become the classical manner of eighteenth-century Virginia. Its H plan suggests the past, but externally the appearance is classical, with round-headed sash windows and doors, bracketed cornice, balconies, and cupola.

The act prescribed that the building "Shall be made in the forme and figure H . . . the foundation . . . shall be four Bricks thick . . . the length of each Side or parte . . . shall be seventy five foot . . . one end of each Part or Side of Which Shall be . . . Semicircular and the lower rooms at the . . . end fifty foot long." A "handsome Staire Case" is specified, and there were to be "great folding gates to each Porch of Six foot breadth . . . the windows to each Story of the Said building Shall be Sash windows and . . . the roofe Shall be a hip roof with Dormand windows." In the middle of the roof there was to be "a Cupulo to surmount the rest of the building Which Shall have a Clock placed in it and on the top of the Said Cupulo Shall be put a flag upon occasion."

Drawings of a simple nature were used by the builders to supplement this detailed description. Succinct but positive reference is made to a "Draught" and "Modell of the said Capitoll." Henry Cary, a builder known also as "Carpenter" and "Overseer," was employed upon his own petition to superintend the work. Shortly afterward the committee for the building authorized "the said Henry Cary to agree with any Capeable pson to make 500000 bricks for the Capitol." Construction progressed so that by July 20, 1703 "That parte that the Corte sitts in is Compleatly finnished on the outside except the Balcony over the Grate doore Comming in on the west side & the lower flower are finished for that the Corte sate there in Aprill last."

The instructions for building were not complete in the original act, and "Further Directions in Building the Capitoll" were incorporated in a supplemental act of August, 1701. It would therefore appear that the design conception for the building was prob-

The ornamental cupola of the Capitol was first of its kind in colonial America.

ably not complete at the outset; alterations were made from time to time, and Cary made many suggestions during the course of building.

Construction of the Governor's House followed, as authorized in 1706. Cary was again asked to direct construction, "to inspect, oversee, and provide for the building aforesaid, with full power to begin, carry on, and finish the same." This building advanced more slowly than the Capitol, in part because of difficulties in obtaining funds. On November 24, 1710 Cary was forced to petition the General Assembly for his full pay of one hundred pounds per annum, owed to him as "Overseer of the building." He declared that the money originally appropriated had long been exhausted, but that he felt himself under obligation to take care of and protect the building in its incompleted condition; he complained that he had been put to considerable expense, and to save himself from ruin had broken up housekeeping at his own plantation and moved his family to the unfinished building, "all of which was very prejudicial."

Governor Spotswood finally brought the building to completion, but not until about 1720. As a reward for his efforts, after rumors of mismanagement, the Burgesses had charged him with "lavishing away the Country's Funds." From this circumstance, and because of elaborate later additions, the House of the Governor came to be known as the "Governor's Palace."

THE ARCHITECT IN VIRGINIA

An architect during the first part of the eighteenth century was known as a "Master Workman; in a Building . . . he who designs the Model, or draws the Plot, Plan, or Draught . . . [and] whose Business it is to consider the whole Manner and Method of the Building." In many instances he was a carpenter or a bricklayer. It is clear that the ability to produce a "draught" was also the accomplishment of an educated gentleman. As an instance, Henry Cary is spoken of as a "Gentleman" as well as "Overseer." Virginia had no practicing architects until after the arrival of William Buckland in 1755 to supervise the building of George Mason's Gunston Hall. Other architects were gifted amateurs; those active in Williamsburg include Thomas Jefferson and Richard Taliaferro. Curiously, however, not a single building of Williamsburg of the eighteenth century can be as-

The Governor's House was described by a traveler as large, commodious, and handsome.

signed with documentary proof to an architect as designer.

In 1772, Jefferson made plans for the completion of the Wren Building as it had been planned, a rectangular building enclosing a quadrangle or court. Part of the foundation for the addition was actually laid before the Revolution put a stop to building operations. Later he drew plans for remodeling the Palace, which, he said, "is capable of being made an elegant seat." These plans also came to nothing, because the building burned in 1781.

THE USE OF HANDBOOKS

The working details used by builders of the early eighteenth century in composing their building de-

signs were obtained from builders' handbooks of which many had been published in London before

To be LET, on Wednesday the 4th of January next, if fair, otherwise next fair day,

THE BUILDING of a STEEPLE to Williamsburg church. All Gentlemen that incline to undertake the same are desired to attend that day at the said church with proper plans, and a just estimate to each plan.

JOHN PIERCE,   ⎱ Church-
WILLIAM EATON, ⎰ Wardens.

The functions of the colonial architect were exercised by gentlemen and builders called "undertakers." The advertisement above is from the *Virginia Gazette* of December 15, 1768.

Features such as cornices, doors, windows, and chimney details were copied from builders' handbooks, but the exterior design of a typical Williamsburg house such as the Alexander Craig was a development of the local carpenter and mason.

1700. These early manuals warrant description. The handbooks informed the builders how to frame a wall or roof, how to produce designs of windows, doorways, balconies, fireplaces, and cornices. A minimum of instruction was given, however, on the "orders of architecture," and no complete designs for buildings were included. Yet with this limited assistance the craftsmen built the Capitol, Palace, and many other early eighteenth-century Williamsburg buildings.

Later, actual designs of buildings were incorporated in more comprehensive publications by such men as James Gibbs, Isaac Ware, William Halfpenny, and Robert Morris. These writer-architects were producers of designs which, to quote Gibbs in 1728,

"would be of use to such Gentlemen as might be concerned in Building, especially in the remote parts of the Country, where little or no assistance for Designs can be procured."

Books on architecture were frequently included on the library lists of residents of Williamsburg. Maurice Evington, a carpenter-builder, advertised in the *Virginia Gazette* in 1779, the sale of "12 or 15 books of architecture, by the latest and best authors in *Britain*, viz *Swan, Pain, Langley, Halfpenny*, &c. &c." George Wythe, with a more scholarly interest, wrote abroad for a copy of Vitruvius in Latin, having the advice of Thomas Jefferson that "the edition of Vitruvius . . . with commentaries by Ticinus . . . is best."

Examples of the principal items in the carpenter's equipment are illustrated below, with their numbers shown at right. For each named example there were many varieties adapted to special uses. Of planes alone, the carpenter often owned thirty or more. Many of these tools were made by the carpenter or by the local blacksmith. 1. *Mallet*, for driving dowels and wedges. 2. Adjustable *Level*. 3. *"Square"* for angles and measuring. 4. *Compass* used as dividers and to inscribe circles. 5. *Screw Driver*, not used much before 1800. 6. *Auger*. 7. *Buck Saw*. 8. Open *Hand Saw*. 9. *Jackplane*. 10. *Molding Plane*. 11. *Claw Hammer*. 12. *Brace*. 13. *Adze*. 14. *Hatchet*. 15. *Gimlet*.

Tools of the pioneer American builders. The tools used by the carpenter in Virginia, two centuries ago, are almost identical with those familiar tools found in the carpenter's chest today.

The Manner of Furnishings

"How much more agreeable it is to sit in the midst of old furniture . . . which [has] come down from other generations, than amid that which was just brought from the Cabinet-maker's, smelling of varnish, like a coffin!"
—*Thoreau*

THE COLONISTS in eighteenth-century Virginia made a deliberate effort to create and maintain an environment comparable to that of England. They kept informed of the latest decorative practices in the mother country and followed them in the treatment of the interiors of their homes and public buildings. Many of the materials for finishing and furnishing these were imported from England, and colonial artisans were in large part trained there. Numerous travelers were struck by the marked similarity of the appointments of Virginia and English houses; a comment made by one visitor about 1755 concerning an ordinary in Leedstown, Virginia, may be taken as typical. "The chairs, Tables, &c of the Room I was conducted into, was all of Mahogany, and so stuft with fine large glazied Copper Plate Prints: That I almost fancied myself in Jeffriess' [in London]."

WALLS, CEILINGS, AND FLOORS

The interior walls of Williamsburg buildings of the eighteenth century were usually plastered, use being made of oyster-shell lime, river sand, and animal hair. The plaster was commonly whitewashed.

Full-length wainscoting or paneling, originally a protection against damp walls, was sometimes used

Opposite, common room for dining, in the Raleigh Tavern.

in Williamsburg homes, as in the Peyton Randolph House, but it was more often employed in public buildings such as the Capitol and the Palace or in the larger mansions of plantation owners. A builder's dictionary of 1774 defines wainscot as "the timber work that serves to line the walls of a room, being usually made in pannels, and painted, to serve instead of hangings." In Williamsburg, the wainscot was customarily of local pine.

A "dwarf" wainscot or dado, carried to a height of from three to five feet from the floor, was more common in both private and public buildings. In some cases where the dado is used, special emphasis is given the fireplace by carrying paneling above it to the ceiling. A fine example of such treatment may be seen on the east wall of the living room of the Brush-Everard House, where also a chair-height wainscot has remained in place since its original installation in the eighteenth century.

A still more frequent wall treatment is that in which paneling is completely dispensed with, leaving only the wood base and cornice and a heavy, waist-high protective molding known as a chair rail. A variety of wall treatments might often be found within a single building; for example, there was ample precedent in the reconstructed Capitol for the use of ceiling-height wainscoting in the Council

Chamber and the Court Room, a dado in the House of Burgesses, and a chair rail only in certain committee rooms.

An eighteenth-century architect-builder, in a discussion of English wall treatments that applies

1.

equally well to Virginia, states that the rooms "were commonly wainscoted quite up to the ceiling, and terminated by a cornice; but later the custom is to carry it only up chair high . . . [whereas] the rest of the wall is covered with flowered paper, which is very

cheap and beautiful, or else it is finished with stucco covered with hanging; to prevent the paper being spoiled by the dampness of the wall, it is pasted on thin cloth, and fixed in frames."

Wallpapers became fashionable in the latter part of the eighteenth century as a substitute for white-washed and paneled walls and because of a desire for added enrichment. The mode at one period favored Chinese designs. The *Virginia Gazette* of December 28, 1769 carried an advertisement that "JOSEPH KIDD, *Upholsterer, in Williamsburg,* HANGS rooms with paper or damask, stuffs sophas, couches, and chairs, in the neatest manner, makes all sorts of bed furniture, window curtains, and matrasses, and fits carpets to any room with the greatest exactness. . . . He also under-

Facsimile of early wallpaper from the Brush-Everard House.

takes all sorts of HOUSE PAINTING, GILDING, and GLAZING; and paints floor cloths, chimney boards, and signs, according to directions."

Records show that wallpaper was used in the Palace. In a letter written on April 15, 1771 to Samuel Athawes, Robert Beverley, referring to the Ballroom, states that "L^d. B. [Lord Botetourt] had hung a room with plain blue paper & border'd it with a narrow stripe of gilt Leather." When the Palace interiors were restored, the walls of the Supper Room were

2.   3.   4.   5.

covered with eighteenth-century paper painted in the Chinese manner, since Chinese patterns were in vogue in England at the time the wing containing this room was added. The Upper Middle Room was hung with tooled and gilt Spanish Morocco leather similar to that mentioned in the journals of the Virginia Council. Damask hangings were a mark of interior elegance that apparently graced fewer Williamsburg homes than did wallpaper. In the Robert Carter House on Palace Green, however, wood strips used to attach the fabric still remain embedded in the plaster walls of certain rooms.

Early eighteenth-century damask at Colonial Williamsburg.

Casement windows with leaded glass were the prevailing window type in Virginia throughout the seventeenth century, and the discovery of lead cames in foundation excavations at Williamsburg suggests that they may have been used there occasionally in the early eighteenth century. Meanwhile, the vertical-sliding "guillotine" window came into favor and soon became the dominant type. Glazing was customary but, because of the expense of imported English glass, not universal. Basement windows had wood frames with square bars, but no provision for glazing, since the damp climate made circulation of air beneath the house a necessary precaution against mold and the rotting of timbers. Window weights of lead, with pulleys, were introduced early in the century although ordinarily only the lower sash was made to operate. The common type of sash window throughout the eighteenth century was, however, without sash weights.

Outside shutters were used on wood-frame structures, whereas in brick houses and public buildings the deep reveals permitted the use of inside or wainscot shutters which folded against the jams. Venetian blinds were introduced into Virginia after the middle of the eighteenth century. The *Virginia Gazette* in 1770 noted that Joshua Kendall, house carpenter and joiner, "BEGS leave to inform the Public that he . . . makes the best and newest invented *Venetian* SUN BLINDS for windows, that move to any position so as to give different lights, they screen from the scorching rays of the sun, draw up as a curtain, prevent being overlooked, give a cool refreshing air in hot weather, and are the greatest preservatives of furniture of any thing of the kind ever invented."

Windows were hung with draperies or curtains of damask, chintz, calico, printed linen, linsey-woolsey, or like materials. In bedchambers these usually matched the curtains of the bed.

Most Virginia rooms of the eighteenth century had a fireplace, since this was virtually the only means of heating at the time. By the latter part of the century a few stoves existed, and one example, the "Botetourt Stove," a cast-iron "ventilating type" which was given to the House of Burgesses and probably stood at one time in the Palace, can still be seen in Williamsburg. The fireplace was usually centered on the side or end wall of the room. Corner fireplaces, however, were more frequent in Williamsburg and Virginia than elsewhere in the colonies. Typically these corner fireplaces were built back-to-back in adjoining rooms, a single chimney serving the pair. Fireplace openings were large at the beginning of the century, tending later to decrease in size both because of the growing scarcity of wood and because improvements in

6.

1. "Dwarf" wainscot, and paneled mantel facing of arched fireplace, Market Square Tavern. 2. Eighteenth-century drawing of Venetian blind (Diderot), 1765. 3. Operation of Venetian blind, window of Chowning's Tavern. 4. Bedroom of the Wythe House, showing eighteenth-century embroidered cotton bedspread made in Virginia, chair upholstered in English crewelwork, and Scotch carpet on the floor. 5. Original wall-height paneling of the parlor in the Peyton Randolph House. 6. The Botetourt Stove, "the newly invented warming machine" considered by its inventor "as a masterpiece not to be equalled in all Europe."

their construction made them more efficient. The openings were spanned by a beam of heavy oak or by a brick arch until the time of the Revolution, after which the iron lintel gradually became common.

Stone for paving and mantels had to be brought to Williamsburg from England or other parts of Virginia and the colonies, since, with the exception of coarse marl rock which was only occasionally used for building, there was none native to the peninsula. William Byrd in 1732 recommended the quarrying of a "white stone" found near Fredericksburg, "appearing to be as fair and fine grained as that of Portland." This stone was used in Williamsburg and elsewhere in Virginia. Marbles and other stones for mantels were not confined to more pretentious buildings like the Palace but were also fairly common in private houses. The ledger of Humphrey Harwood, a Williamsburg carpenter-mason, records the following bill to Mrs. Betty Randolph, the widow of Peyton Randolph: "Decr. 2 [1778] To Repairing marble Chimney Piece 12/ [shillings]," and in 1790 occurs this entry in the account of John Blair, Esq.: "To setting up 2 grates (one very large)—taking down the marble-mantel-piece and taking up the Hearth—& relaying them 18/." The marble mantels found today in the Peyton Randolph and John Blair houses, it is believed, are the very ones mentioned in Harwood's account book.

Most mantel facings were of wood, and these were sometimes incorporated into the paneling of the room or combined with overmantels. The woodwork was separated from the fireplace opening by a plastered brick "frame" of varying width. A hearth of brick or, quite frequently, English Purbeck or Portland stone, was provided.

Exposed beam ceilings had prevailed in the colony throughout the seventeenth century, but by the close of the first quarter of the eighteenth century ceilings of residences in Williamsburg were almost without exception lathed and plastered, for, as is noted in *The Builder's Dictionary* of 1734, experience revealed that "The Plaistered Ceilings so much used in England, beyond all other Countries, make by their whiteness the Rooms so much Lightsomer, and are excellent against raging Fires. They stop the Passage of the Dust, and lessen the noise over head; and in Summertime the Air of a Room is something the cooler for them, and in the Winter something the

1.

2.

1. Eighteenth-century paneled wood mantel, John Blair house. The plastered brick frame and curved back of the fireplace are typical early details. 2. Marble mantel reproduction, George Wythe House. 3. Original marble mantel, east room of the Peyton Randolph House.

Opposite page, examples of colonial glassware.

3.

Warmer, because it keeps out cold Air better than the Board-floors alone can do."

The use of stone floors was restricted to public buildings; the Purbeck stone of the Capitol and Palace is notable. Brick and brickbat floors and pounded clay were commonly found in kitchens and other dependencies. Aside from this, however, flooring was universally of local yellow pine, usually 1¼ inches thick and laid in from 5- to 10-inch widths in edge grain; this was laid without underflooring and generally face-nailed.

Rugs, as we speak of them today, were used sparingly on these floors, but English and Oriental types, and needlepoint, were employed. Until almost the middle of the eighteenth century carpets mentioned in records were used primarily as coverings for tables and bureaus; the turkey carpet specified for the table of the Council Chamber of the Capitol is a conspicuous example. Later, carpets as floor coverings came into vogue, along with painted floor cloths; both were advertised for sale in Williamsburg. Turkey, Wilton, and Scotch carpets were among other types used. Among the papers of John Norton & Sons, merchants of London and Virginia, is an invoice of August 14, 1769 listing, together with other articles to be sent "by the first Ship for York River," to Mrs. Martha Jacquelin "2 Kilmarnock [Scotch] Carpets, 1 large & 1 small [and] 1 painted duck Floor Cloth." Painted floor cloths were cheaper substitutes for carpets and may be considered the

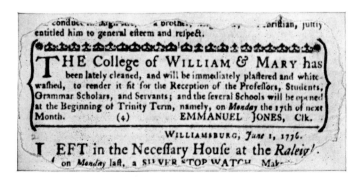

forerunners of our linoleum and oilcloth. They were made of stout canvas coated with oil paint and printed with a pattern, and were generally used on

stairs and in halls and rooms of lesser importance. Rush mats were also in use throughout the century.

PAINTING AND THE USE OF COLOR

In eighteenth-century Virginia, the range of colors from which the painter could choose was restricted compared to the wide variety at his disposal today. Paints were purchased in England, and numerous invoices, letters, and advertisements have provided reasonably complete information as to paint ingredients available at the time. For example, William Allason, a wholesale merchant of Falmouth, Virginia, from 1760 to 1790, lists in his "invoice book" such inventories as:

> On hand—Copperas, 16 pounds
> Indigo
> Light Blue
> Chalk
> 10 Casks White Lead
> 1 Cask Red Lead
> 1 Cask Spanish Brown
> Red Paint from Maryland
> Linseed Oil, 10 gall.

These ingredients and certain others such as burnt umber, yellow ocher, orpiment, verdigris, litharge, Spanish whiting, lime for whitewash, archil, and walnut oil constituted the palette with which the colonial painter worked.

In those days painters used both oil and water paints. Linseed oil, made of ground flaxseed, and oil of walnut were the vehicles used in oil paints. Although both of these were produced in the colony, they were also frequently imported. Of the two, walnut oil was the first to be used, and it was considered better than linseed oil for interior work, "for Lindseed Oyl within doors will turn yellow, and spoil the beauty of it [the paint]; which . . . Walnut-Oyl . . . prevents; for that makes it keep a constant whiteness." Oil of turpentine, a rapid-drying spirit obtained from native yellow pine, was often used as a thinner.

The speaker's chair in the House of Burgesses, Capitol, was in the original building.

White lead (carbonate of lead), called a body pigment because it forms the bulk of the paint, was, in colonial times as today, a primary ingredient of oil paints. There were two chief varieties, one called ceruse, which was the purest and cleanest sort, and the other simply white lead; a third, flake white, is spoken of as scarce and dear, "to be found only under the Lead [roofs] of some very old Buildings, where time has by the assistance of some sharp quality in the Air, thus reduced the undermost superficies of the Lead." The color pigments, reds, blues, greens, yellows, and browns, were derived from natural earths (Spanish brown, burnt umber, yellow ocher); from metals (copperas, verdigris, orpiment, and red lead); and from plants (indigo and archil).

Whitewash, a water paint, was made in the eighteenth century, as it is now, by slaking quicklime in water. The limewash was often colored by the addition of various pigments. Copperas (sulphate of iron), for example, was added to make it green; ocher, to give it a yellow hue; and archil, a color obtained from the liverwort plant, to produce a deep blue tone. Archil, once employed by the Romans, had been used in England since the Middle Ages to decorate the inside walls (and occasionally the outside stonework) of houses. Milk and buttermilk, furthermore, were occasionally used as vehicles in these color washes.

Walls and ceilings in eighteenth-century Virginia were commonly whitewashed; or the wash was sometimes colored. Annual whitewashing was the rule, although it might be done more often as a sanitary measure. The exteriors of frame buildings were likewise frequently whitewashed during the colonial period, as were brick structures late in the eighteenth century. In the case of brick buildings, the lime wash served more than a decorative function, since it formed a hard, crystalline coating on the brick and helped to preserve it. Whitewash continued in use throughout the century, as indicated by a notice of 1792 in the *Calendar of Virginia State Papers* "that Dabney Minor be directed to whitewash the Pedestals upon the top of the Capitol [in Richmond], &

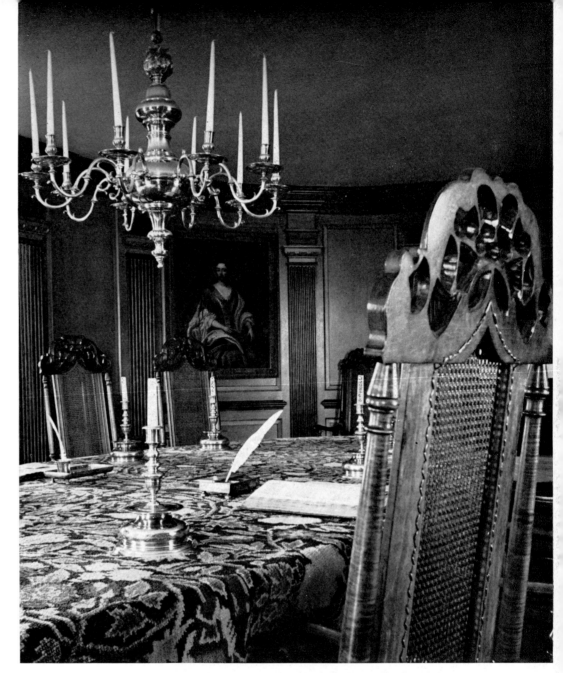

Upstairs in the Capitol is the Virginia Council Chamber. The painting is of Queen Anne.

the Pilasters with Stone Lime, with a mixture of Lamp black to give it the resemblance of stone."

Of the oil colors used in exterior painting in Williamsburg during the eighteenth century, Spanish brown was a favorite. John Smith, philomath, an early authority on house painting, characterized it as "a dark, dull red, of a Horse-flesh colour, 'tis an Earth, it being dug out of the ground, but there is some of it of a colour pleasant enough to the Eye . . . 'tis of great use among Painters, being generally used as the first and primary colour, that they lay upon any kind of timber work, being cheap and plentiful." Spanish brown served on occasion as the finish coat both in interior and exterior work, and it is likely that many Williamsburg houses were of this color. Other colors much in vogue during the first half of the eighteenth century for exterior and interior woodwork were lead color, made of a mixture of indigo and white, and stone color, a white with a slight bluish tint. If the accounts of travelers of the time are to be accepted, however, white was the prevailing color for house exteriors in Williamsburg. Though fences were generally whitewashed or painted, evidence indicates that they were sometimes coated with pine tar as a protection against the weather. One writer of the time, in fact, states that "The common peoples houses . . . [in Virginia] are in general tarr'd all over to preserve them instead of Painting."

Interior woodwork was occasionally left in a natural state, but more often it was painted. Stone and wood colors, Spanish brown, and white were favorites for window frames and bars, doors, stair rails and balusters, mantels, paneling, cornices, and other trim.

Marbleized Wood Baseboard. Photograph of actual eighteenth-century example.

Greens were also used and, of these, verdigris, a green made of copper rust and inclining to bluish, was considered the best and most useful. It was this color, or one like it, that was used to produce some of the familiar blue-green colors of Williamsburg. Shades of yellow and "timber" colors, colors used to imitate the tones of natural woods, vied with these in popu-

larity. Frequent mention is made, for example, of "wainscot" color, umber mixed with white in imitation of oaken wainscot. Olive wood was simulated by ocher, mixed with a little white, veined over with burnt umber; walnut, by burnt umber and white, with veining of burnt umber and black. These last two imitations are early instances of graining. Other popular methods of finishing interior woodwork were: the painting of wainscoting, doors, and other

trim to resemble marble—a treatment known to have been specified for the Council Chamber and other parts of the Capitol; painting to imitate tortoise shell; and staining. Skirting (baseboards) was customarily painted black in Virginia.

Much of the furniture of the eighteenth-century living room or parlor, that "fair lower room designed primarily for the entertainment of company," was comparable to that in our own houses. A spinet or harpsichord, for example, took the place of our piano, and a barrel organ (the record-player of the day) might have been found. Despite the vehement objections of such strict moralists as the Reverend William Stith, who preached before the General Assembly in 1752 on "The Sinfulness and pernicious Nature of Gaming," a drop-leaf card table for piquet or dice often stood in readiness against one wall. The fireplace had its complement of "fire-dogs" (andirons), tongs, shovel, and bellows, a chimney board to close the fireplace opening when not in use, and possibly an adjustable embroidered screen to protect the face from the direct heat of the fire. Other furnishings might include a writing table equipped with a pewter inkwell, quill pens, and blotting sand; a snuff-box; a small locked cabinet for valuables; and a family Bible in its sturdy box, together with a few other books such as a copy of Warner's *Almanack, A Treatise on the Diseases of Virginia*, and *The Young Man's Best Companion*. Looking glasses were a favorite wall decoration; the living room would possibly have had a facing pair on opposite walls. Pictures were less numerous than today, but there might be a few engravings hung on the walls of the living room and other rooms, together possibly with a map of Virginia, a family portrait or two executed by some artist temporarily resident in Williamsburg, and, if the house were that of a wealthier person, a few paintings imported from England or Italy. Matthew Pratt, itinerant American "Portrait Painter, lately from England and Ireland, but last from New York," announced in the *Virginia Gazette* in 1773 that he had "brought with him to *Williamsburg* a small but very neat Collection of PAINTINGS, which are now exhibiting at Mrs. VOBE's near the Capitol; among which are . . . a very good Copy of *Corregio's* ST. JEROME.

. . . VENUS and CUPID, the only Copy from an original Picture by Mr. *West*. . . . A HOLY FAMILY. . . . A copy of *Guido's* JUPITER and EUROPA. . . . FLORA, a Companion to the above . . . [and] a very fine FRUIT PIECE."

The dining room in its furnishings was much the same as that of today. Food had to be carried to the house from an outside kitchen, however, and for this reason trivets, used in rewarming hot dishes, were kept at the fireplace. Other dining-room accessories often seen in the eighteenth century but rarely found today included pewter plates, sometimes with hot-water reservoirs to keep the food warm, napkin presses, knife boxes, tea caddies, spice chests in which the rarer luxuries were kept under lock and key, and horn tumblers, less expensive and more durable than glass. A corner cupboard might hold and display the fine porcelains, glass, pewter, and silver plate of the household, and a wine cellaret was indispensable.

Cooking was almost always done in buildings separate from the main house to reduce the fire hazard, to keep odors and excess heat from the house, and to segregate the slave kitchen help. The character of these kitchens was far different from those of today, because the food was cooked over an open flame in the great fireplace or in an oven actually built into the side of the chimney. Cooking over an open fire required cranes and spits, together with skillets and other cooking utensils with long handles. Kitchen equipment included many ingenious devices, such as automatic spits, toasters, reflector ovens, waffle irons, coffee grinders, roasters, and mixers, which were the forerunners of twentieth-century appliances. Utensils were of wood, pewter, brass, copper, and bell metal, as well as of iron and tin. Candle molds, butter churns, wine presses, and sausage machines were cus-

tomary kitchen and service equipment. Each large house had an outside dairy, and a smokehouse for the curing of meat.

The bedchamber contained one or more four-poster canopied beds, with draw curtains to keep out draughts. A low trundle bed on casters occasionally stood beside the master bed and could be rolled under it when not in use. Bedding usually consisted of feather or flock mattresses, quilts, blankets, and sometimes hemp, canvas, or linen sheets. Closets, an innovation of the eighteenth century, were usually inadequate; large paneled wardrobes or presses, high

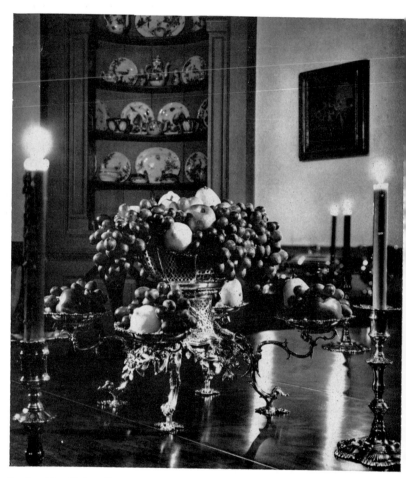

Early English silver epergne and candlesticks, with built-in corner cabinet, dining room of the George Wythe House.

boys, low boys, chest-on-chests, and trunks had to be provided.

Bed warmers, foot warmers, braziers, and other supplementary heating devices were found in all houses, and cast-iron backs were used in fireplaces to protect the brick from the heat. These fire backs, originally a utilitarian feature, became objects for decorative treatment and were ornamented with coats-of-arms, Biblical themes, and other subjects. The chief source of lighting was the candle, made both of the wax of the bayberry and of tallow. Chandeliers, sconces (with silver or mirror reflectors), candelabra, and individual candlesticks were provided to hold them. Hurricane shades of glass were used to shield the candle flame from draughts.

Hurricane Candle Shade.

Illumination was far from adequate by today's standards; the Palace, even when fully candle-lit for a splendid ball or banquet, would have appeared dimly lighted to a twentieth-century spectator. Philip Fithian, writing in his journal of a sumptuous dinner at Nomini Hall, remarked that "The room looked luminous and splendid; four very large candles burning on the table where we supp'd, three others in different parts of the Room." Betty lamps and similar devices burning oil and fat were apparently seldom used in Virginia. A more primitive and cheaper source of light than candles was rushes dipped in scalding fat or grease. One ingenious practice of the time was to whitewash the cheeks and backs of fireplaces to reflect the light of the fire and aid in the illumination of the room. This was especially effective when pine knots, which produce a brilliant flame, were burned.

THE FURNISHING OF EXHIBITION BUILDINGS

In furnishing Exhibition Buildings, Colonial Williamsburg has been guided by documentary evidence as well as by close study of eighteenth-century furnishings and accessories. Inventories have been invaluable, especially at the Raleigh Tavern and the Palace. Public records, diaries, and correspondence have also revealed clues. Since original pieces specified in documents were rarely available, antiques similar to them were substituted, or, in exceptional cases, reproductions were authorized.

At the Capitol much of the required furniture was of such a type or was needed in such quantities that antique equivalents could not be obtained. Authentic reproductions were therefore made to represent the pieces originally in the building. Many antique pieces were also used, however, and the speaker's chair in the House of Burgesses is the very chair which stood in this hall in the eighteenth century. All of the paintings and books are antique.

The furnishings in the Palace are predominantly English, representing the various fashions found in the building during its existence. They are antique throughout except for two of the three magnificent crystal chandeliers in the Ballroom, which had to be specially reproduced. The search for authentic pieces, which still continues, has often been prolonged and far-reaching. It is usually successful, however; for example, eleven Chelsea figures mentioned in an inventory entry have been placed in the Dining Room and ten of eleven have been found for the Parlor.

In the house of George Wythe, a native Virginian, antiques of American origin predominate as contrasted with the English pieces found in the governor's home. No inventory of the Wythe House exists, so that those of comparable houses were followed. Styles of the late eighteenth century are here mingled with earlier pieces. Although no independent furniture forms were developed in Virginia and the pieces show a direct relationship to English prototypes, many of them have been modified by the colonial cabinetmakers.

RECIPE FOR COOKING VIRGINIA HAM

The following recipe is written on the flyleaf of a Bible that belonged to Colonel William Byrd of Westover.

To eat ye Ham in Perfection steep it in Half Milk and half water for Thirty-six hours, and then having brought the Water to a Boil put the Ham therein and let it Simmer, not boil, for 4 or 5 Hours according to size of the Ham—for Simmering brings ye Salt out and boiling drives it in.

The Gardens of Williamsburg

*God Almightie first planted a Garden. And
indeed it is the purest of humane pleasures.
It is the greatest refreshment to the spirits of
man; without which Buildings and Palaces are
but grosse handy-works. . . .*
　　　　　　　　　　—Francis Bacon, *Of Gardens*

Most of the original colonial gardens of Williamsburg had disappeared before their restoration was begun. Portions of old walks, fences, walls, remnants of boxwood hedges, some outbuildings, and other evidences of old gardens, however, still existed. These, along with listings of plant materials preserved in diaries, letters, and other records, served as a basis for restoring the gardens.

Eighteenth-century gardens in Williamsburg were formal in treatment and, since they were designed as an integral part of the original plot plan, may be looked upon as architectural in character. The plan of the grounds, or place layout, was carefully considered from the beginning, and its various features—the outbuildings, gardens, and connecting walks—were brought into a relationship with the house that was both satisfying aesthetically and sound from the standpoint of use. The dependencies were never directly connected with the house in this region where the winters were mild, and the warm, humid summers made ample circulation of air important. Typically, a kitchen, dairy, smokehouse, and well were placed about an outside working area or service court paved with brick or marl, at the side or rear of the main house. A stable and coach house with an area for maintenance work and a paddock were generally located at the back of the lot.

When the main house was situated on a street corner, a special type of plan layout was occasionally developed. Here, since access to the property could be gained from the side street, stables, storehouses, and other service buildings were placed along this street. Thus the house with its dependencies took the form of an L.

Between the various oubuildings or beside them were placed the kitchen and pleasure gardens. At times they were combined in one planted area of flowers, vegetables, and fruit, but more often they were kept separate.

The individual designs for the pleasure garden were carefully adapted to the topography, size, and shape of the area and were either central or axial in type. In the central plan, areas of planting— square or rectangular, wedge-shaped, round, or oval beds—were grouped about or radiated from a central point. The axial plan usually featured a long central walk intersected by cross walks which divided the garden into a series of squares or rectangles.

Garden walks were usually of brick or marl, but other surfacing, such as washed pebbles, gravel, broken pieces of stone, oyster and scallop shells, and brickbats were common. As a general rule, early designers were practical in their arrangement of service walks, which were laid to connect work areas in the most direct fashion, with few deviations for the sake of design. In the pleasure areas, however, where balance and form took precedence, the contrary was true.

Few indications of the existence of ornamental garden features have been found in studying records and archaeological remains. The Palace gardens, however, did make relatively extensive use of elaborate gates, decorative piers and termini, vases, steps, seats, arbors, garden houses, enclosing walls, and clairvoyees (openings affording a vista through high walls). The smaller gardens achieved interest, for

Prentis House Garden Plan. **A typical arrangement of planted area with house and outbuildings.**

the most part, through balanced outbuildings, walks, decorative fences, and seats. European precedent in the use of stone or lead figures and fountains was apparently disregarded.

Fences, so familiar in the Williamsburg scene today, were required by colonial law to be built around each lot. An act of the General Assembly of 1705, designed to protect the gardens from stray horses and cattle, required the owner of every half-acre lot contiguous to Duke of Gloucester Street to "inclose the said lots, or half acres, with a wall, pails, or post and rails, within six months after the building, which the law requires to be erected thereupon, shall be finished." The height of the fence was set at four and one-half feet. Another act, applying to the colony in general, permitted the substitution for the fence of a so-called "quick-set" hedge. Such hedges, or "live fences," were made by digging a ditch and planting a quick-growing shrub on the top of the soft ridge of earth thrown up at the side.

Brick walls with molded brick copings were, in the town itself, usually confined to the enclosure of the grounds of public buildings. Post and rail fences and paling (picket fences) specified in the act became typical for private gardens, and fences of wattle (woven twigs) were also found. The "worm" or "snake" fence was frequently used to enclose fields in and about Williamsburg; this was a fence without posts made of six- or eight-foot rails laid zigzag fashion with ends interlocking—the familiar "Virginia rail" fence which continued in common use until replaced by wire fencing near the end of the nineteenth century.

PLANT MATERIALS

Of the trees and shrubs grown in the colonial gardens, some were imported at various times and others were native to Virginia. Hedges of imported boxwood were popular and widely used, not only because of their beauty but also because they grew slowly and required infrequent clipping. More rapidly growing shrubs needed constant attention to prevent them

The design of the Custis-Maupin Garden is a modified British flag.

from clogging the paths and overshadowing the adjacent beds. Holly hedges and trees were also found in the gardens of Williamsburg; although some of this holly was brought from England, it was transplanted with difficulty and most of the old specimens are native. Records show that English yew was brought to Virginia in the hope that it would make satisfactory hedges, but the colonists found the climate usually too dry to permit it to flourish. Both hawthorn and privet were imported and used in creating quick-set hedges.

Among flowering shrubs which in recent years grew extensively in Williamsburg, forsythia has been removed from the restored area since it was found to have been introduced in the nineteenth century. The flowering quince ("japonica"), once removed for a like reason, is being reinstated; research established that it was introduced shortly before 1800.

Of the trees seen by the visitor, perhaps the most striking is the paper mulberry with its complex of gnarled trunks and its pulpy outer shell. It is a popular misconception that these trees were used in the colonial silkworm industry; the silkworm was actually reared on the true mulberry, the black and white. A number of true mulberry trees are to be found in Williamsburg, one of the finest being the ancient gnarled tree which overhangs the east wall of the Capitol.

Prominent among ornamental trees used by gardeners of the eighteenth century were the mimosa, with its fern-like leaf, and trees noted for the beauty

> GENTLEMEN and others, may be supply'd with good Garden Pease, Beans, and several other Sorts of Garden Seeds: Also, with great Choice of Flower Roots; likewise Trees of several Sorts and Sizes, fit to plant, as Ornaments in Gentlemen's Gardens, at very reasonable Rates, by Thomas Crease, Gardener to the College, in Williamsburg.

of their flowers such as the dogwood, Southern magnolia, red bud, and catalpa. The crape myrtle was introduced from India shortly before 1750. Trees widely used and honored for their shade were the elm, sycamore, tulip poplar, and pecan. The *Juniper virginiana*, commonly called red cedar, was traditionally used as a border along either side of plantation approaches, and avenues of these may still be seen throughout Virginia. Of these trees, the mimosa and crape myrtle were imported; the others were native to the region.

Fruit trees were important in Williamsburg gardens. Governor Nicholson, in laying out the town in half-acre lots, specified that each person should have sufficient ground for his house, his garden, and orchard. Fruit had been useful to the settlers of Virginia from the outset. "Fruit growing in early colonial days," says S. W. Fletcher, in *A History of Fruit Growing in Virginia* (1932), "was chiefly for the purpose of securing a supply of 'most excellent and comfortable' drinks. . . . We have the word of Captain John Smith that 'few of the upper class planters drink any water.'" The first colonists found in abundance palatable small fruits such as grapes and berries: wild strawberries, huckleberries, blackberries, and raspberries. Of the tree fruits which the land afforded, the crab apple was small and bitter, the wild cherry practically worthless, the plums inferior in quality to European sorts, and, as for the persimmon, Captain Smith wrote "if it be not ripe it will draw a man's mouth awrie, with much torment." There were no native pears or peaches, and these, together with the apple, quince, plum, cherry, apricot, and nectarine were introduced from Europe. In the eighteenth century, fruit was frequently used in making liquors—wine, cider, perry (pear cider), peach brandy, and other fermented fruit juices.

Trees were of still more vital importance to Williamsburg and the colonies as the source of the raw materials for building, cabinetmaking, and the production of household utensils. Cedar, cypress, yellow pine, oak, elm, and beech were used in building, whereas walnut, the "cabinetmaker's wood," together with pine, cherry, applewood, and holly for inlay work, were employed in furniture manufacture. Farm implements were fashioned of wood (oak, ash, and hickory), often to the complete exclusion of any metal, leather, or fiber. Household manufacture of wooden ware achieved a high development as a craft. Poplar, ash, and alder were used to create objects of grace and endurance such as spoons, ladles, churns, buckets, trays, milk pails, and many other articles of domestic use.

In a day when chemical dyes were largely unknown, dyes for the coloring of cotton, linen, and wool were obtained directly from plant materials. The barks, roots, and leaves of trees as well as berries and flowers were sources of dye colors. Many varying shades of blue, for instance, were obtained from the indigo plant, and the madder vine gave a wide range of shades from turkey-red to pink. Among the colors derived from barks were yellow and dark brown from the black walnut; golden brown from chestnut oak; green from hickory; black from willow; and gold from the black oak. The sumac berry yielded gray, and the petals of the poppy were a source of crimson.

A sunk fence or "ha-ha," a common enclosure of plantations, so devised as not to interrupt the view toward river or countryside.

These were but a few of the many colors made from plant materials in the eighteenth century. Certain of these dyes were produced in quantity and exported from the colony, whereas others, such as a black made from logwood and a reddish brown from brazilwood, were derived from imported woods. Natural dyes are still made by native craftsmen in the highlands of southern Virginia and North Carolina and are considered by many superior to more commonly used chemical colors.

JOHN CUSTIS AND HIS GARDEN

A Williamsburg garden which no longer exists but which was, nevertheless, one of the best known in Virginia, was that of Colonel John Custis, father-in-law of Martha Dandridge Custis, who became the

"Quick-set" hedge, an enclosure made by digging a ditch and planting the mound thus produced with a quick-growing hedge.

wife of George Washington. Custis, a Councilor of the colony, built a house with a large garden in Williamsburg when he found that his home at Arlington on the Eastern Shore was too remote from the city. He was an eager student of the ways of nature and a lover of all growing things; he labored for twenty years in his garden, furnishing it with all manner of plants, trees, and shrubs, many native to the new country and many imported from England and elsewhere.

Custis apparently began his gardening venture in 1717, because in a letter of that year to his merchants in England he wrote: "I have lately got into the vein of gardening and have made a handsome garden to my house; and desire you will lay out 45 [£] for me in handsome striped hollys and yew but most hollys." A large proportion of his plant materials succumbed on the way to Williamsburg, and in later letters he complains bitterly about the lack of care used in their packing and the stupidity of ship captains who allowed them to die on the way: "The box[wood] for my garden was all rotten as dirt did not save one sprig; the gardener was either a fool or a knave and by his management never packed anything before to go beyond sea."

There was an unlimited variety of fence and gate posts in Williamsburg.

Sir John Randolph of Williamsburg was instrumental in bringing Custis in touch with Peter Collinson of London, a wool draper whose hobby was gardening and whom years of experiment had made an expert botanist and naturalist. Collinson was deeply interested in the flora and fauna of the colonies and had become acquainted with several Americans, including William Byrd of Westover, who sent him plants and seeds from their gardens. A few extracts from letters written by Custis to Collinson in 1735 give an idea of the plants exchanged and a glimpse into the Custis garden: "I have planted the Pistacious Nutts and I think I shall allmonds. I have allmond trees that thrive well, but they bloom so early that it is not once in a great many years but the frost kills the blossoms. . . . I have planted the dates, but I doubt they are too tender to do well here. I have planted the seeds of the Cedar of Lebanon. . . . As for those peas you call Italian beans we call them black eyed Indian peas, and I make yearly hundreds of bushels of them and ship them to the West Indies."

Among Collinson's American friends was John Bartram of Pennsylvania, a farmer who became one of the country's greatest naturalists and whose garden on the Schuylkill near Philadelphia was one of America's first botanical gardens. Acting at the suggestion of Collinson, Bartram toured Maryland and Virginia, stopping off in Williamsburg to make the acquaintance of John Custis. Custis later wrote Collinson of the visit of the famous naturalist: "He [Mr. Bartram] is the most taking facetious man I ever met with and [I] never was so delighted with a stranger in all my life. I have had a letter from him . . . with his kind offers to send me some Dutch white currant bushes which would be very acceptable."

Thus Custis became acquainted with Bartram, and a triangular correspondence among three of the greatest gardeners of the day was begun. Two, Collinson and Bartram, left behind gardens which have become public property and which are preserved in honor of their creators. Of the Custis garden nothing remains which can with certainty be said to have been planted by his hand. However, near

Early in the century hedges were squared and shrubs clipped into artificial shapes.

the Custis Kitchen, the only one of his buildings which still exists, there stands an old yew tree which may well be a survivor of those which he planted and tended with so much care.

THE RESTORATION OF THE GARDENS

Plant materials other than trees, bulbs, and a few shrubs do not survive a century unless carefully tended. When trees and hedges from original plantings do survive, as in the case of the old boxwood of the Brush-Everard garden, they have proved a valuable aid in determining the original design pattern of the garden.

Archaeological studies, in the course of which known sites of old gardens were excavated and examined, have been of great assistance in restoration work. Features of the original landscape plan, such as remains of outbuilding foundations, brick and marl walks, paved service areas, surface drains, and old wall and fencepost lines, have often been uncovered. In many cases, walks found several inches below the surface revealed the main garden axis, size and shape of planting areas, and the general lot layout.

Additional information on the arrangement of gardens and outbuildings was found through research into old records such as insurance policies, which frequently included sketches of the lots; descriptions

in travel accounts and old letters; eighteenth-century maps of the town such as the Frenchman's Map; and nineteenth-century photographs. Finally, study of surviving remains of gardens in the surrounding Tidewater region and of the Sauthier plans of North Carolina towns of the eighteenth century has been of great assistance in determining detail design of the plantings as well as the general character of the garden designs.

EXAMPLES OF GARDEN LAYOUTS

The Wythe Garden

The site plan of the George Wythe House and outbuildings is an example of an L-shaped scheme. Service structures and their surrounding yards have been placed along the side street. Following traces revealed by excavation, a main axial walk with parallel side paths and a lawn terminating in a low mound and arbor have been developed at the rear of the house. Balancing small outbuildings accent the farther corners of the mall, much as the great North Garden of the Palace is terminated by necessary houses (the eighteenth-century privy).

Fruit and kitchen gardens along one side of the central mall balance the service areas along the other. Vegetable and fruit-tree plantings are interwoven, and fig bushes have been used along one side of the garden. A small herb plot south of the main house is enclosed with box hedges accented at the corners by topiary specimens (shrubs clipped in various shapes).

The Bryan Garden

The Bryan House layout is typical of plans in which the pleasure garden is located at the side of the house. The plan follows the usual colonial pattern, with the kitchen, smokehouse, and service area located at the rear of the house and the stable yard with its paddock at the back of the lot. The intervening space between kitchen area and stable yard has been developed as a small kitchen garden, whose four plots would be of sufficient size to supply "sallots," herbs, and vegetables.

The pleasure garden has been patterned after

Fruit trees and topiary lend vertical accents to the formal design of the Bryan Garden.

examples illustrated in the Sauthier maps, in which a square or circular central design is often shown. In the Bryan garden, central and axial layouts have been combined, but from the street this garden appears axial, featuring a live oak, arch, and seat at the south. Along its minor cross axis the garden appears as a central type, with its square center and four topiary pieces the most conspicuous objects.

The Palace Gardens

The Palace layout is as formal and elaborate as the furnishings and architecture of the Palace itself; this was one of the earliest of the great formal gardens of Virginia, being preceded and rivaled in extent and elegance only by Governor Berkeley's garden at Green Spring. The influence of the Palace garden is evident in many plantation gardens.

The forecourt design, with its four oval planting beds, stone walks, narrow entrance gate, and curved enclosing walls, is clearly indicated in the Bodleian Plate, an eighteenth-century copperplate discovered in the Bodleian Library at Oxford. The service yard, to the west of the west flanking building, contains the buildings necessary for the maintenance of a large household—kitchen, scullery, salt and meat houses, smokehouse, laundry, and related outbuildings. This noisy, active area was placed as far away from the governor's living apartments as demands of service would permit.

The boundaries of the Ballroom Garden were discovered by excavation of long-hidden wall foundations. The main building axis and foundations of the north gate set the line for the broad central walk. The position of the main cross walk, likewise, was fixed by the east and west gate foundations. The detail design of the diamond-shaped parterres (ornamental arrangements of beds or plots) was adapted from those shown on the Bodleian Plate. The lead vases were listed in Palace inventories.

The North Garden continues at a slightly lower level on either side of the main central axis. This is planted in typical early eighteenth-century topiary, pleached arbors, and tulip beds so important in Dutch-influenced schemes. The architectural enclosure of brick walls with interspersed piers, the elegant iron-work of gates, grilles, and clairvoyees, the steps and decorative piers with lead vases, and the corner necessary houses, are all fundamental component features of the design.

At the east of the Ballroom Garden is the plain parterre or tree-box garden, and at the west a box garden laid out in a quadrangle of squares and circles. This adjoins the Revolutionary burying ground, in which the bodies of 156 soldiers were found.

To the north of the burying ground is a fruit garden enclosed by a brick wall, against which figs are espaliered. Nectarines are trained on wooden supports and the exotic pomegranate grows in the fruit garden. Behind the garden are the holly Maze, patterned after that at Hampton Court, England, and the Mount, a terraced mound of earth in the shape of a truncated pyramid, with a flight of steps leading to a platform at the top. Both the Maze and the Mount are late seventeenth-century landscape features.

The Restoration of an American Town

*"He who alters an old House is ty'd as a Trans-
lator to the Original, and is confin'd to the
Fancy of the first Builder. Such a Man would
be unwise to pull down a good old Building,
perhaps to erect a worse new one."*
—*Builder's Dictionary, 1734*

THE RESTORATION of Colonial Williamsburg represents the first attempt on a large scale to recover the physical form and atmosphere of an entire colonial town. This project has been undertaken with the conviction that our old buildings with their furniture and implements are the visual memorials of our early history—"the scene and witness of human adventures and events." It was the realization that a wealth of historic fact and artistic value lay hidden in the venerable remains of Williamsburg which led to its restoration.

Only recently has America come to recognize the cultural values in its past architecture, although historic buildings have always had their loyal protectors. Mount Vernon, Independence Hall, and the Old State House at Boston were early accepted as historic monuments, as well as many other significant buildings in all sections of the country. Inexperience or misdirected enthusiasm sometimes led to faulty restoration work which caused even more damage to a building than indifference or neglect; but gradually there has grown up a tradition of preserving the original expression as well as the actual physical structure of buildings.

What has come to be called the restoration of ancient buildings owes something to the architect Thomas Ustick Walter, designer of the great dome of the National Capitol. Walter, who was perhaps America's first "restorer," was asked by a building committee to make changes to the interior of old Christ Church in Philadelphia, in the year 1834. Before accepting the commission, Walter remarked to the sponsors: "I have often looked with regret at the

innovations on the purity of the architecture of Christ Church. The propriety of reducing the height of the ceiling and making it a flat surface has now been suggested. This would make the house easier to speak in, and it could be warmed with more facility; but this alteration would completely ruin the architecture of the building, and destroy all that dignity and ecclesiastical effect so completely attained in this venerable fabric."

It was at almost this same time—in 1838—that Bruton Parish Church in Williamsburg was considerably "renovated," and not with the whole-hearted approval of all parishioners. Miss Elizabeth Galt of Williamsburg, who was visiting in Brooklyn at the time, wrote Dr. D. D. Galt in 1840 to inquire, "And do tell me, who have been the Goths and the Vandals who have modernized our dear abbay?"

Since then, many organizations have been formed for the care of historic buildings and to arouse public interest in their behalf. Many of these are local or regional in character. The Mount Vernon Ladies' Association, founded in 1853, is an early example. This association acquired Mount Vernon in 1858 from John Augustine Washington, Jr., who had tried without success to interest the United States Government in purchasing it as a national monument. In Virginia, the Association for the Preservation of Virginia Antiquities has joined with state and local groups to protect historic sites. At Williamsburg, this society kept secure the foundations of the colonial Capitol, deeding them to its restorers when reconstruction was begun. The APVA, which has worked closely with the Williamsburg project from the start, also owns the site of the Magazine, which is now leased to Colonial Williamsburg.

Other societies worked on a national scale. The American Scenic and Historic Preservation Society was organized in 1895 and has pioneered in stimulating interest in America's architectural past. Another example is the Committee on Preservation of Historic Monuments of the American Institute of Architects, established in 1909. One of the most recent organizations formed on this nationwide basis is the National Trust for Historic Preservation, chartered by act of Congress in 1949. Supported entirely by the contributions of member organizations and individuals, it serves both as a clearinghouse of information and an advisor on problems of historic preservation. The Federal Government, in the Historic Sites Act of 1935, declared it "a national policy to preserve for public use historic sites, buildings and objects of national significance for the inspiration and benefit of the people of the United States." A year earlier, in 1934, the National Park Service initiated a major project with the establishment of a Historic American Buildings Survey to record, photograph, and make measured drawings of historic structures. This, and a companion study also dating from the thirties —The National Survey of Historic Sites and Buildings—were resumed with new vigor under the broad Mission 66 program of the National Park Service. The purpose has not been to acquire these places, but to point out the desirability of preserving them.

Throughout America, attempts to restore or preserve significant buildings and historic sites have become more frequent in recent years. Two of the best-known restoration projects were carried out in Virginia at Monticello and Stratford. Both are contemporary with the restoration of Colonial Williamsburg. Monticello was purchased by the Thomas Jefferson Foundation in 1929 and restored soon afterwards. Stratford Hall, in Westmoreland County, Virginia, home of Robert E. Lee, was a larger undertaking. This property was conveyed to the Robert E. Lee Memorial Foundation in July, 1929. It was restored under the direction of Fiske Kimball, architect, in 1932-1935. The work done included the repair and preservation of the mansion and its dependencies. The gardens and orchards were also restored.

Early drawings of Williamsburg, early maps, inventories, land grants, newspaper advertisements, records of loss by fire, early insurance policies, all were considered in the process of restoration. The engraving above was made at some time prior to 1875.

THE RESTORATION OF WILLIAMSBURG

The recovery of colonial Williamsburg was undertaken in fulfillment of a plan proposed to the late Mr. John D. Rockefeller, Jr., by Dr. W. A. R. Goodwin, late rector of Bruton Parish. This plan was almost prohibitively ambitious. Its realization was made possible only by vast expenditures and the continuing and undiminished interest of the donor. The first steps in acquiring houses and lots and in developing the initial organization were taken in 1926.

The purpose of Colonial Williamsburg at the outset was to recover the significant portions of a historic and important city of America's colonial period. This purpose, always flexible in nature, has come to have a much broader significance. Not only are the buildings the subject for study, but also the life and thought associated with them. A new emphasis is placed upon the significance of the painstaking craftsman. In addition, a program of interpretation has been developed, based on the recognition of Williamsburg's importance in the formulation of American political thought, in education, commerce, fashions of the New World, and as a seat of religion.

The program, as it has been carried out, involved more than the repair and restoration of existing colonial homes and buildings. Many buildings, including the immensely significant Capitol and Palace, had disappeared, and had to be completely reconstructed on their original foundations. Authentic furnishings and decorations were required. Gardens had to be replanted.

To accomplish this, it was necessary to purchase or control virtually all the area that formerly comprised the colonial city. A vast staff of experts was employed: architects, archaeologists, landscape gardeners, builders, town planners, historians, lawyers, engineers, and many others. The architectural firm of Perry, Shaw and Hepburn was retained in 1927 to have direct charge of the architectural development and the manner of restoration. Their valued services continued until 1934 when a local architectural staff, headed by A. Edwin Kendrew and Singleton P. Moorehead, was formed at Williamsburg to carry to completion the original restoration program and to maintain the buildings already erected and their gardens. Perry, Shaw and Hepburn still serve in an advisory capacity. Arthur A. Shurcliff, the landscape architect who at the outset directed the landscape restoration and city planning for the project, also continued as a consultant until his death in 1957.

For the first two years the chief problem was that of research. Archives in America and Europe were

Courtesy of the Massachusetts Historical Society

Measured drawing of the Palace, made by Thomas Jefferson, probably in 1779. This drawing was of great value to the architects in developing an authentic plan arrangement and in rebuilding the Palace.

searched for any record or reference that would aid the restoration work to follow. Supplementary archaeological evidence was sought. During this research stage, a number of extraordinary discoveries were made. In the Bodleian Library at Oxford, for example, an eighteenth-century copperplate was found on which were shown, as carefully engraved illustrations, the first Capitol at Williamsburg, the Governor's Palace, and the buildings of the College of William and Mary. This engraved plate was of great assistance to the architects in composing their designs, and is now on exhibition in Williamsburg. Two drawings

The Bodleian Plate (see page 45). This engraved plate showed the Palace, the Capitol, and the College of William and Mary in their eighteenth-century appearance.

Wood engraving of the Apollo Room at the Raleigh Tavern, made in 1848. This engraving indicated an early architectural treatment of the room.

The Prentis Store was stripped of its additions and restored.

RESTORATION

This photograph shows the John Crump House before the turn of the century. Built in stages during the 1700's, the house had as many as three tenants at one time.

A water-color drawing of the Greenhow-Repiton House. The house, demolished several decades ago, was reconstructed with the aid of this drawing.

An old photograph of the Scrivener House gave a clear picture of its early architectural appearance.

by Thomas Jefferson were added to the pool of reference material. One was a scale drawing of the Governor's Palace which was obtained from the collections of the Massachusetts Historical Society and which supported the archaeological basis for the reconstruction of the plan of the Palace; the second, located at the Huntington Library in California, was a carefully drawn proposal for the extension of the Wren Building at the College of William and Mary. Some years previously, a minutely detailed map of Williamsburg, probably drawn in 1782 and attributed to an

prompted by the enthusiasm of draftsmen in the employ of the architects. To co-ordinate and interpret the architectural and historical material, a separate Department of Research and Record was formed. When the scope of work began to include building interiors and furnishings, the assistance of specialists in interior architecture was called upon by the architects. Mrs. Susan Higginson Nash directed the furnishing of the Exhibition Buildings, a work later carried on by Curators James L. Cogar, 1931 to 1948, and John M. Graham II, 1948 to 1970.

The Frenchman's Map is so called because it is believed to have been made by a French Army map maker in 1782. It was an invaluable aid in the restoration of Williamsburg, since it shows with accuracy the plan of the town and location of buildings and their property lines, existing after the Revolution.

anonymous French engineer, had been found in an antique shop at Norfolk and presented to the College. This map, which came to be known as the "Frenchman's Map," proved an invaluable aid, since it shows the position of buildings of the town during the Revolutionary period. Additional military maps and surveys, prepared by French, English, and other army officers during their sojourn in Williamsburg at the time of the Revolution, were helpful.

The supervising architects at first were fully occupied with the design of buildings to be reconstructed and restored and in making measured drawings and photographs of plantation houses and gardens of the surrounding Virginia area. Much of the field work was

During the first full work year (1928), a committee of advisory architects, consisting of eight men with special competence in colonial architecture, was appointed. Although advisory in nature, this group passed on all plans and designs, as well as on the use of precedent. In the course of their periodic meetings, a code of restoration principles and procedure was compiled which has served the architects as a guide:

1. All buildings or parts of buildings in which the colonial tradition persists should be retained irrespective of their actual date.

2. Where the classical tradition persists in buildings or parts of buildings, great discretion should be exercised before destroying them.

3. Within the "restoration area" all work which no longer represents colonial or classical tradition should be demolished or removed.

4. Old buildings in Williamsburg outside the "restoration area" wherever possible should be left and if possible preserved on their original sites and restored there rather than moved within the "area."

5. No surviving old work should be rebuilt for structural reasons if any reasonable additional trouble and expense would suffice to preserve it.

6. There should be held in the minds of the architects in the treatment of buildings the distinction between *Preservation* where the object is scrupulous retention of the surviving work by ordinary repair, and *Restoration* where the object is the recovery of the old form by new work; the largest practicable number of buildings should be preserved rather than restored.

7. Such preservation and restoration work requires a slower pace than ordinary modern construction work, and a superior result should be preferred to more rapid progress.

8. In restoration the use of old materials and details of the period and character, properly recorded, is commendable when they can be secured.

9. In the securing of old materials there should be no demolition or removal of buildings where there seems a reasonable prospect that they will persist intact on their original sites.

10. Where new materials must be used, they should be of a character approximating the old as closely as possible, but no attempt should be made to "antique" them by theatrical means.

To put these procedures into practice was often difficult. It is hard to tamper with an old building without destroying the attraction acquired by age. At the same time it is an accepted principle that parts must be repaired and known original details should be restored, such as in window sills and moldings, where sufficient fragments still exist. Repairs and cleaning-up add to the worth of an old building when these are done in a workmanlike manner that is obviously protective. "The best repair," according to Philip Webb, founder of England's Society for the Preservation of Ancient Buildings, "is a sort of building surgery which aims at conservation."

STEPS IN RESTORATION

In Williamsburg the restoration of a building is undertaken according to well-established procedure.

Drawing of the Capitol on Bodleian Plate.

The house to be restored is first examined under the direction of architects and draftsmen familiar with colonial building construction and design. To prepare the house for this preliminary study, the building is cleared of all vines; near-by shrubbery is removed. In some cases, trees must also be relocated. Grass around the foundation is cut back and convenient access made to all walls. Where necessary, walls in danger of collapse are shored up; inside floors are given support. Debris is removed from the house and all floors made "broom clean."

Measurements are then made of the interior and exterior of the house, including floor heights from basement to roof, and the relationship of floor heights to the outside grade. Sketches with measurements are drawn of walls, brickwork, floors, partitions, ornamentation, stairs, mantels, and windows and doors along with their framing. Wall surfaces are examined and special attention is given any evidence of changes or relathing. Color samples are obtained from the layers of paint. In the study of the foundation a record is kept of any deterioration, rotted sills, closed windows, and parts added or removed. Photographs, now including motion pictures, are periodically made of the restoration process to serve as a field record.

On most sites, archaeological excavations are carried out in a search for further evidence of the nature of the structure and its date. Diggers probe buried foundations, older wall footings, brick or marl garden paths, and drainage ditches. The soil is sifted for fragments of tile, brick, pottery, metalwork, glass, stone, and other artifacts that may shed a possible light on the form or use of the building.

Sometimes it is necessary to strip a part of the facing of the house down to the framing, in order to observe changes and examine its physical condition. This process of stripping has always been done with great caution and only where imperative. Old flooring and original window frames, even when partly rotted, are left alone. Rather than undertake a drastic replacement of the whole, repairs are made on whatever parts are splintered or decayed. Weatherboarding in bad condition is extremely difficult to put in a state of

EXCAVATED FOUNDATION OF
THE GOVERNOR'S PALACE

The Palace floor plan was revealed by painstaking excavation at the site. The completeness of the plan is shown by the drawing and photograph at the left, with original existing walls indicated in solid black in the drawing. The photograph above shows paving both of Purbeck marble and of brick.

sound repair. In some instances the existing weatherboarding, even though recent, is preferred to the complete smoothness of new siding.

When first-hand scrutiny of the house is completed, scale drawings of the structure are made. Modern additions are removed. An authentic sash replaces the modern sash found in place. The original cornice is restored, perhaps by following the profile of parts concealed beneath an added porch. Foundations are underpinned, and sills and window framings repaired.

In the meantime, research assistants have painstakingly gathered existing data on the history of the house, its owners or tenants, its use, and possibly even its appearance and the materials of which it was constructed. This information is derived from county records, town maps, abstracts of title, wills, inventories, and even advertisements from the local *Virginia Gazette*.

After this preliminary research and investigation is completed, work is begun. Of course, all of the missing evidence is rarely discovered: the age of a building or its additions is elusive, and the problem of replacing missing parts is often difficult.

The techniques for preserving, restoring, or reconstructing the buildings of Colonial Williamsburg have been developed through experience. New techniques are constantly being evolved. But the methods used for this work are always subordinate to the spirit of the whole undertaking—an attempt to recapture with authenticity the environment as well as the physical form of a small American town of two centuries ago.

A Photographic Tour of Williamsburg

These variously shaped roofs are those of the dependencies grouped about the service court of the Palace.

The illustrations that follow serve as preparation for seeing the town, as a helpful accompaniment to a walking tour, and as an accurate record of what has been seen in Williamsburg.

THE GOVERNOR'S PALACE

One approaches the Governor's Palace from Duke of Gloucester Street by way of a stately avenue bordered by catalpa trees. During the times of the royal governors, displays of fireworks were on occasion held here and in 1776 it was used as a parade ground.

The Governor's House, ironically called the "Palace" because of the funds lavished upon its construction, was "a magnificent Structure, built at publick Expence, finished and beautified with Gates, fine Gardens, Offices, Walks, a fine Canal, Orchards, &c . . . by the ingenious Contrivance of the most accomplished Colonel Spotswood."

The Palace in colonial days was the scene of splendid social gatherings. At the yearly celebrations of the king's birthday, for example, it is said to have presented an appearance equalled and surpassed only by the Court of England. Inventories of the governors give ample evidence of the elaborateness of the Palace furnishings. In addition to furniture provided by the colony, the "standing furniture" of the Palace, each governor brought a large collection of his own. The Palace furniture ranged in character from the "newest fashion" of Governors Botetourt and Dunmore, to some items characterized by observers as "old fashion'd."

At right, Supper Room, showing Chinese influence. Below, left, English chandelier of same room. Below, right, puzzle, "The Kings and Queens of England."

Right, Little Dining Room, used by the governor and his family. About the mahogany Chippendale table is a particularly fine set of Queen Anne chairs with original needlework seats. The tea set on the mantel is Whieldon agateware, and the bowl on the table is Lambeth Delft.

Below, right, detail of mantel of Little Dining Room, and left, detail of mantel of Bedchamber over Parlor.

Opposite, the Parlor, where small groups of guests could be received and entertained. Chelsea figures adorn the mantel. The tea and coffee service is Worcester; the silver teakettle was made in London in 1747.

The Brush-Everard House, a stone's throw from the Governor's Palace, is almost as old as the town itself. John Brush, first keeper of the Powder Magazine, purchased the lot in 1717 and finished building the original house while the Palace was being completed. The house was probably expanded about mid-century by Thomas Everard, clerk of York County. Though not wealthy, Everard was a man of comfortable, middle-class circumstances. The restoration reflects his period of ownership.

The library has been compiled from a list of volumes selected by Thomas Jefferson for a friend who described himself as unacquainted with the classics and without time "for any intricate or tedious study."

THE GEORGE WYTHE HOUSE

George Wythe, an eminent lawyer who became the first professor of law in an American college, was also a signer of the Declaration of Independence. The youthful Jefferson frequently sat at his table, along with other students of the college, and learned lessons in the rights of man.

The house was large for Williamsburg but strikingly austere in its balanced architecture. Its design is credited to Richard Taliaferro, Wythe's father-in-law. The house plan is the "center hall" type, two rooms deep. Its gardens and outbuildings are arranged similarly to those of a small plantation.

The southeast bedroom of the Wythe House. The cherry chest-on-chest was made in New England in the mid-eighteenth century. The window and bed hangings are cotton resist dyed in two shades of blue. The table at the right is a forerunner of the modern dressing table. Gentlemen's wigs were placed on wig stands and powdered.

The student's room of the Wythe House. On the oval gateleg table are a terrestrial globe and a portable orrery. The mahogany table with Spanish feet holds a number of objects that might have been used by students in the eighteenth century. The microscope at left, made in London about 1725–30, stands in front of its case.

THE JAMES GEDDY HOUSE
AND SILVERSMITH SHOP

The Geddy house was erected about 1750, partly on foundations of an earlier structure owned and occupied by James Geddy, Sr., gunsmith. Its low-pitched roof without dormers makes it an architectural rarity in Williamsburg.

The younger James Geddy, silversmith, lived and worked here through the middle years of the eighteenth century. He and his brothers, who were brass founders, cutlers, and blacksmiths, helped greatly in the twentieth-century re-creation of their workshops by scattering around the premises a veritable treasure of debris—and some silver spoons—to be unearthed by today's archaeologists.

A present-day successor pauses in his task of hammering out a silver bowl to contemplate the honorable history of his craft.

Opposite page, Bruton Parish Church

61

The Magazine was built in 1715 to protect the arms, gunpowder, and ammunition of the colony. Lord Dunmore's secret removal of the powder the day after the battle of Lexington caused the first assembling of an armed force in Virginia for what was to become the American Revolution.

Mortars and gunpowder in barrels were stored on the ground floor of the Magazine (left) and the armorer had a shop in the front. To protect the Magazine, which was considered "much exposed," a high brick wall was built around it and, near by, a Guardhouse.

The Courthouse on Market Square, erected in 1770, is now used as an Archaeological Museum. Four Doric columns, added to the portico after a fire in 1911, were omitted in the final restoration of the building in 1932.

Courthouse during the 1870's.

Courthouse as restored after fire.

In the corner of the Raleigh taproom is a reproduction of an eighteenth-century bar.

RALEIGH TAVERN

At this tavern the leading patriots of Virginia are recorded to have gathered, before the Revolution and afterward, including George Washington, Patrick Henry, Thomas Jefferson, George Wythe, Peyton Randolph, George Mason.

Termed "the second capitol of the colony" because lawmakers convened here on several occasions after the Assembly was dissolved by an irate governor, in 1769 it was the scene for discussion and formulation of the non-importation agreement. In 1774, an influential group of patriots met at the Raleigh to issue the call for the First Continental Congress.

WETHERBURN'S TAVERN

Henry Wetherburn, who for a time was host at the Raleigh Tavern, moved across the street and opened a rival hostelry in the earliest part of this building (to the left of the tree) about 1740. He added the extension to the right about ten years later, and the structure has been in continuous use ever since.

The room-by-room inventory made at the time of Wetherburn's death served as a principal guide in furnishing the restored tavern with antique articles similar to those listed. The inventory indicated that the tavern-keeper could make a total of nineteen beds available in rooms upstairs and down.

66

The Capitol was one of the principal buildings of colonial America. Of two capitol buildings that stood successively on this same site, the first (built 1701-05) was selected for reconstruction. At right, Conference Room.

General Court of the Capitol, above. This paneled room was set apart for the use of the General Court; across the hall was the office of the Secretary of the Colony.

Less imposing in architecture was the House of Burgesses, said to be similar in its appearance to the House of Commons of the mother country. The House of Burgesses, the Council, and the General Court of the Virginia colony met at the Capitol from 1704 to 1776.

Lowering the flag at the Capitol.

Not far from the Capitol was built a Public Gaol, described as "a strong sweet Prison." Stocks and a pillory were required to be near the prison.

Opposite page, a common cell and leg irons.

At mid-century, Williamsburg was spoken of as offering an "agreeable residence." Most of the houses were of modest size, commonly a story and a half in height, with steep gabled roofs. These dwellings were generally framed with wood, "cased with feather-edged Plank, painted with white Lead and Oil, covered with Shingles." The illustration is of the Greenhow-Repiton House.

The Mary Stith Shop, one of the many modest buildings on shaded Duke of Gloucester Street, now contains an itinerant musician's room.

A SELECTION OF SMALL HOUSES

The gambrel roof became extremely popular in Williamsburg. Here are shown the Lightfoot House, at left; the Tayloe House, below left, and, below right, the Orrell House. These houses are similar in their common possession of a side hallway, corner fireplaces with chimneys contained within the outside walls, and construction of wood frame, faced with weatherboards.

Opposite page. The upper illustration shows the Waters-Coleman House, with an exceptionally fine pair of brick chimneys. Sloped-roof closets of brick occur at each end of the front. This, and the Moody House, lower left, and the Travis House, lower right, have long sloping roofs at rear.

The Orlando Jones House (above), with its kitchen at the right, viewed from the garden side. The covered porch entry and chamber above are features found in early Virginia houses, notably Bacon's Castle.

The John Blair House (left) was at the time of the Revolution the home of John Blair, Jr., a Virginia delegate to the Constitutional Convention and a Justice of the Supreme Court of the United States. The plan of the house originally consisted of a center hallway and entrance with a room on either side. It was later lengthened and a second doorway added.

The illustration on the opposite page shows the western doorway of the John Blair House with stone steps said to have come from the first theater in Williamsburg.

Mary Stith Tin Shop, above, devoted to the manufacture and sale of household accessories made of tin. The unusual roof overhang, running the length of the building, serves as both a sun shade and a rain shelter.

Allen-Byrd House. This, at one time, was the town house of William Byrd III. Surrounding the house were extensive gardens including "beautiful crape myrtles and pomegranate bushes."

St. George Tucker House, one of the few large houses of the town. Soon after the Revolution it became the home of St. George Tucker, second professor of law at the College of William and Mary.

The Semple House has a unique two-story center pavilion and balanced wings.

The older part of the Coke-Garrett House was erected prior to the Revolution. The goldsmith, John Coke, lived in it at one time. Its fine west staircase, shown above, is in what was popularly known as the Chinese Chippendale manner.

A shop, with separate entrances, was at one end of the James Anderson House. It adjoined the two-story main house, at right.

The Brick House Tavern was reconstructed on old foundations. York County land records were of assistance in determining the floor arrangement.

The James Anderson House is most notable for its associations with George Washington, a frequent visitor to Williamsburg. On November 5, 1768, he wrote in his diary, "Dined at Mrs. Campbell's, where I had spent all my Evenings since I came to Town." Mrs. Christiana Campbell kept this house as a tavern for a short time. The house has been reconstructed.

The Deane House, above, situated on the Palace Green, was for a while the home of Elkanah Deane, coachmaker, formerly of Dublin.

The Robert Carter House, at left, was the town house of Robert Carter of Nomini Hall. It was given special prominence by its location next door to the Palace and for a brief period served as the house of the Royal Governor.

The Peyton Randolph House, of distinguished architectural simplicity, was at one time the home of Peyton Randolph, first president of the Continental Congress; it has been identified as the headquarters of General Rochambeau in 1781; General Lafayette was entertained here on the occasion of his visit to Williamsburg in 1824.

Josiah Chowning's Tavern, built on the site of an early inn.

KITCHENS AND OTHER

Kitchens were placed away from the house as a protection from the heat of cookery. Here are shown: 1. the Robert Carter Kitchen; 2. the John Blair Kitchen; 3. the Ludwell-Paradise Kitchen; 4. the Talia-ferro-Cole Kitchen; 5. the Bryan Kitchen.

1.

2.

3

4

5

84

OUTBUILDINGS

View of roofs of the Archibald Blair outbuildings at right.

Below, left, Wythe House outbuildings. The coach house of the Ludwell-Paradise House is shown below right.

Above, fences and yards near Taliaferro-Cole Kitchen.   *Opposite page*, Robertson's Windmill.

Fences were a concern of the inhabitants of Williamsburg almost immediately following the laying out of the streets and town by Francis Nicholson, Lieutenant Governor of Virginia. In 1705 persons building on the Duke of Gloucester Street were asked to "inclose the said lots . . . with a wall, pails, or post and rails, within six months after the building . . . shall be finished." The enclosure by fences was required to keep stray cattle from destroying the gardens.

The "palisade fence" with "pickets" was most common. A second kind of fence was made of posts and rails. Even the snake fence, native to this colony, was probably used to enclose near-by fields and is associated with the day when timber was still abundant. It was termed the "ne plus ultra" of fences, in later days called the Virginia rail fence. It required no posts but an abundance of split rails. It extended in zigzag lines in sublime disregard of the waste of land occupied by its wanderings. It is probable that a few of these fences were built here. Some owners of lots chose to enclose their houses and gardens by what was termed a "quick-set" hedge, planted on a mound thrown to one side by digging a ditch as a border.

ARTS AND CRAFTS

In Williamsburg during colonial days there were skilled craftsmen in many trades. Sixteen cabinetmakers and upholsterers were engaged from time to time in the making and repair of furniture. Coachmakers, gold and silversmiths, gunsmiths, mantua makers, hairdressers, carpenters, joiners, masons, blacksmiths, and farriers, all appear in York County records as having followed their trades in the town or locality. Extracts from the *Virginia Gazette* give an overall picture of local arts and crafts. November 28, 1745: *"Richard Caulton,* Upholster, from *London,* gives this public Notice to all Gentlemen, Ladies, and others, That he doth all Sorts of Upholsterer's Work, after the newest Fashion. . . . at reasonable Rates. . . ." July 25, 1766: *"B. Bucktrout,* Cabinet Maker, from London, on the main street near the Capitol in *Williamsburg,* makes all sorts of cabinet work, either plain or ornamental in the neatest and newest fashions. . . ."

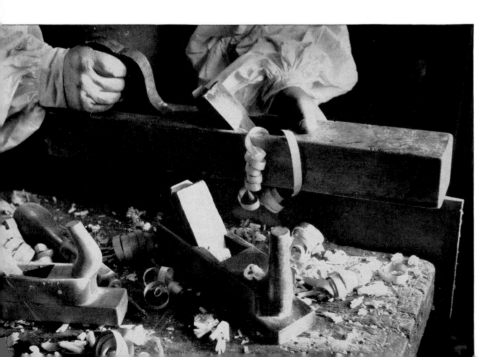

Photographs at left show a craftsman today using tools of two centuries ago.

Hay's Cabinetmaking Shop. By 1756, when he bought the buildings that stood on this site, Anthony Hay was an established cabinetmaker. His activities were not limited solely to the practice of his trade, for he would also repair furniture and make coffins. In time an addition to the shop was built, spanning the creek on brick piers. The interior is shown at right. Below are the tools of cabinetmaker and joiner.

The Sign of the Rhinoceros.

Boot and Shoemaker's Shop.

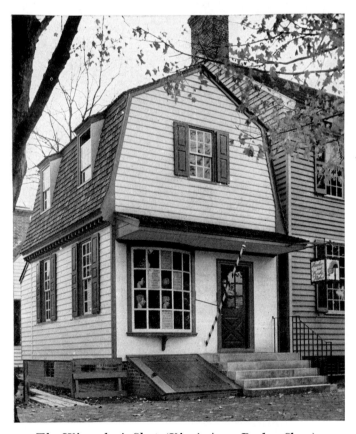

The Wigmaker's Shop (King's Arms Barber Shop).

Display window of the Wigmaker's Shop.

Shop of Elkanah Deane, coachmaker, an emigrant from Ireland, who advertised in 1767 the making of "ironwork of every kind relative to the coachmaking trade."

Deane was also a skilled wheelwright, who repaired pleasure carriages "in the best manner."

THE COLLEGE OF WILLIAM AND MARY

The College of William and Mary, founded by royal charter in 1693, is, after Harvard, the oldest college in the country. It was an English college set down in the wilderness of America with an educational system patterned closely after those of England. Three chief purposes motivated its establishment, "the education of the white youth of Virginia, the training of ministers for the church and the conversion of the Indian heathen." The illustrations show: 1. The statue of Lord Botetourt, an ardent supporter of the College. Of this famous statue, which once stood in the portico of the Capitol and now stands in the Earl Gregg Swem Library, the *Virginia Gazette* noted, " 'tis much admired by all the curious and artists." 2. The Wren Building, the oldest academic structure in British America, was begun in 1694 and burned three times between 1705 and 1862. 3. The Great Hall, the one-time refectory of the College. 4. The President's House, erected in 1732. 5 and 6. Two views of the arcaded porch at the rear of the Wren Building, originally intended to face a courtyard.

MERCHANTS SQUARE

Before the restoration of the town, all stores, legal offices, garages, and other business properties were scattered in haphazard fashion up and down Duke of Gloucester Street.

With a new town plan, the architects restricted most business buildings to the western end of the main street, and located them in such a way as to interfere as little as possible with the restoration of the town. The future growth of the town was kept in mind, with the thought that such growth could take place laterally along the side streets.

Above, shops and offices are grouped in a business district just west of the restored area. Buildings are designed in the style of Virginia Tidewater architecture.

Below, a section across the western end of Duke of Gloucester Street showing the Wren Building beyond, on the axis of the street, and the stores and shops of the business district at either side. The shops are set back at certain points to such an extent that the combined width of the sidewalks flanking the street is nearly double the width of the street.

94

The plan of the shopping area (right) shows the generous width of the main street and the flanking sidewalks, and the passageways connecting the latter with the inner block parking spaces at the rear of the business buildings.

FEATURES OF THE BUSINESS AREA

A spacious and shaded shopping district resembling, somewhat, the appearance of a colonial village square.

Shops are not crowded, shoulder to shoulder in a straight row, but are irregularly placed, with passages between certain of the buildings to shaded parking areas at the rear.

Pedestrian access to the stores is from the brick paved walks on the main street. Shoppers coming by car can park in the areas provided for that purpose and enter some of the stores directly from the rear.

The building exteriors, while not replicas of eighteenth-century prototypes, do conform in their architecture to the building manner of Tidewater Virginia in the eighteenth century.

THE INFORMATION CENTER

Key building among Colonial Williamsburg's visitor facilities, the Information Center is located on a forty-acre tract outside the restored area. The special space requirements of twin theatres and extensive exhibition areas called for a building in free architectural style to accommodate the size and relationship of these spaces. Visitors are invited to leave their automobiles at the Information Center and begin their tour of Williamsburg by boarding special buses at the lower level of the building.

Within the Information Center a continuous program of films, lectures, and exhibits orients the visitor to Williamsburg and suggests to him a variety of experiences that can deepen the meaning of his visit to the restored capital of Virginia.

ABBY ALDRICH ROCKEFELLER
FOLK ART COLLECTION

In addition to the eighteenth-century restored area, the Abby Aldrich Rockefeller Folk Art Collection is a major point of interest for visitors to Williamsburg. Located on the grounds of the Williamsburg Inn, this separate museum houses one of the finest collections of folk art in America. The handsome brick building is designed in the style of the early nineteenth century, with Flemish-bond brickwork, stone trim and quoins, wood modillion cornice, and semi-circular stone arched doorway.

An oval garden enclosed by a serpentine wall provides an attractive approach to the building. A stone terrace is adjacent to the main entrance, which is decorated by wrought-iron gates. The interior architecture provides a harmonious background for the collection.

BIBLIOGRAPHICAL NOTES

Colonial Williamsburg: Its Buildings and Gardens is based upon early historical works on Virginia, together with researches in the field of American architecture over a period of years. Sources of information and recommended authorities for extended reading are listed in the following notes. Footnotes to quotations in the text have been omitted for ease in reading. Few attempts have been previously made to assemble a listing of the scattered literature on the preservation and restoration of old buildings. The titles on this subject collected here will assist, it is believed, in the formulation of an improved and uniform restoration practice, with benefits from the extensive experience of other countries.

HISTORICAL BACKGROUND

Early writers on Virginia make scant mention of architecture, but they do supply a detailed picture of the historical background and life in the colony. Among the works of that time may be cited Robert Beverley, *The History and Present State of Virginia* (London, 1705; Chapel Hill, 1948); Hugh Jones, *The Present State of Virginia* (London, 1724; Chapel Hill, 1956); and *Journal & Letters of Philip Vickers Fithian, 1773-1774: A Plantation Tutor of the Old Dominion,* Hunter D. Farish, ed. (Williamsburg, 1957). A secondary work by Philip Alexander Bruce, *The Economic History of Virginia in the Seventeenth Century* (2 vols., N.Y., 1895) is most helpful on the economic life of the opening years of Virginia colonization. T. J. Wertenbaker, *The Old South; The Founding of American Civilization* (N.Y., 1942), gives an interesting and humanized account of Virginia history including extensive references to its early architecture and crafts. Some of the statements of Lyon Gardiner Tyler, *Williamsburg, the Old Colonial Capital* (Richmond, 1907), have since required revision, but the book should be read for the picture it gives of pre-restoration Williamsburg. Indispensable is Rutherfoord Goodwin's *A Brief & True Report Concerning Williamsburg in Virginia* (Williamsburg, 1941). The author has gathered together most of the pertinent documentary references to the town. The book summarizes facts related to the town's restoration and offers its own account of Williamsburg history.

Topics on Virginia history, personalities, trades, and materials can be traced to Virginia magazines and legis-lative sources with the aid of Earl G. Swem's invaluable *Virginia Historical Index* (2 vols., Roanoke, 1934-36). The rich store of material concerning eighteenth-century Williamsburg and Virginia contained in the *Virginia Gazette* has now been made conveniently available by the Institute of Early American History and Culture, which has prepared a detailed index for the years 1736-80. The files of the Departments of Research and of Architecture of Colonial Williamsburg offer compiled information on house histories, materials, building practices, and personalities of eighteenth-century Tidewater Virginia.

ARCHITECTURE AND GARDENS

Williamsburg architecture and gardens must be studied in relation to the region, also as a part of a development in America. R. A. Lancaster, *Historic Virginia Homes and Churches* (Philadelphia, 1915), is one of the better works for illustrations of notable plantation houses and gardens. Fiske Kimball, *Domestic Architecture of the American Colonies and of the Early Republic* (N.Y., 1927), is the most reliable guide for general study of early American architecture. *The Mansions of Virginia* by Thomas T. Waterman (Chapel Hill, 1945) is a well-illustrated work that discusses the Palace and many of the lesser dwellings of Williamsburg. A series of Williamsburg Architectural Studies was inaugurated in 1958 with Marcus Whiffen, *The Public Buildings of Williamsburg* (Williamsburg, 1958). This comprehensive presentation of Williamsburg's public buildings was followed by a companion volume by the same author, *The Eighteenth-Century Houses of Williamsburg* (Williamsburg, 1960). The latter study includes detailed descriptions of the original houses in the town. The first illustrated discussion of the restoration of Colonial Williamsburg appeared in *The Architectural Record*, LXXVIII, 356-458, December, 1935; also LXXXII, 66-77, October, 1937. Illustrations in *The Record* are by the photographer, F. S. Lincoln. Samuel Chamberlain, *Behold Williamsburg: A Pictorial Tour of Virginia's Colonial Capital* (N.Y., 1947) is comprehensive and has informative captions. In *Brothers of the Spade* (Worcester, 1949), Earl G. Swem brought together the horticultural correspondence of Peter Collinson and John Custis from 1734 to 1746. Raymond L. Taylor has catalogued eighteenth-century Williamsburg flora in *Plants of Colonial Days* (Williamsburg, 1959). See also Mary Frances Goodwin, "Three Eighteenth Century Gardens," *Virginia Quarterly Review*, X, 218-33, April, 1934; a typescript of Joseph Prentis' Garden Book, March 1784-February 1788, in the Library of Colonial Williamsburg; S. W. Fletcher, *A History of Fruit Growing in Virginia* (Staunton, 1932); Edith Tunis Sale, *Interiors of Virginia Houses of Colonial Times* (Richmond, 1927); *Gardens of Colony and State*, Alice G. B. Lockwood, ed., Garden Club of America publication, Vol. II (N.Y., 1931-34); *Historic Gardens of Virginia* (Richmond, 1923), compiled by the James River Garden Club, Edith T. Sale, ed.; E. M. Betts, *Thomas Jefferson's Garden Book* (Philadelphia, 1944); and "The Gardens of Williamsburg," a manuscript monograph by Alden Hopkins, late Resident Landscape Architect of Colonial Williamsburg (Williamsburg, 1949).

The Historic American Buildings Survey (in the charge of the Library of Congress) has undertaken the creation of a permanent graphic record of the existing remains of early dwellings in America. This has become a notable and extensive source of photographic illustration of early buildings, as well as of measured drawings of many examples.

RESTORATION OF OLD BUILDINGS

There are several works that deal with the manner in which old buildings should be preserved or restored. J. Thomas Schneider prepared a comprehensive mimeographed report in 1935 for the Department of the Interior, Washington, D.C., titled *Report to the Secretary of the Interior on Preservation, Restoration and Reconstruction of Historic Sites and Buildings*. The purposes and methods of preservation are therein outlined, including a résumé of the methods and experience of foreign countries. The League of Nations (International Museum Office) issued a useful document in Paris in 1933 which deals with principles of preservation, as applied to national monuments, *La Conservation des Monuments d'Art & d'Histoire*. *Reports of the Society for the Protection of Ancient Buildings* (London, 1909-40) contain "principles of preservation and restoration." Paul Clemen, *Kunstschutz im Kriege* (Leipzig, 1919), is a study of the preservation and restoration of churches and other art monuments injured by war. *Historic Preservation Today* (Williamsburg, 1966) contains a number of thoughtful and informative papers, and comments on them, delivered at an international seminar on historic preservation held in Williamsburg in 1963. *The Restoration Manual* by Orin M. Bullock (Norwalk, Conn., 1966)

is an excellent illustrated guide to the principles and practices that should govern the restoration and preservation of old buildings. Attention is also called to three lesser works on restoration, originating in Great Britain. William Harvey, *The Preservation of St. Paul's Cathedral and other Famous Buildings*, is termed "a text book on the new science of conservation" (London, 1925). Albert R. Powys, formerly Secretary of the British Society for Protection of Ancient Buildings, is author of an excellent working manual on *The Repair of Ancient Buildings* (London, 1939). There is more sentiment and less of experience in Walter Hindes Godfrey's *Our Building Inheritance, Are We to Use or Lose It?* (London, 1944). The National Trust for Historic Preservation, Washington, D.C., should be consulted for guidance on questions pertaining to methods of building preservation or restoration.

PRESERVATION OF OUR ARCHITECTURAL HERITAGE

Since the end of the last century the doctrine of preservation has been gradually replacing that of restoration alone. The principle, which has become a sort of international code, is that historic buildings require and deserve preservation and care.

Old buildings in Williamsburg which have been preserved are important for two, sometimes overlapping, reasons. The first is their design and fitness of purpose. The other is their association with past life and history. This second quality varies and has been acquired slowly. Because of this association each building has been a source of new interest and delight to viewers. In this way a "patina" has been built up. This romantic quality has little to do with the rules of proportion and architecture, but it does evoke the past: the people and the way they lived, dressed, and conducted themselves.

It has been held important here at Williamsburg that we keep in mind this dual nature of the old buildings. Forgetting this in the restoration, we might destroy the patina of association and its indigenous significance and leave only the building's renovated shell. To touch an old building at all without destroying its charm and authenticity is exceedingly difficult. Three centuries ago John Dryden in *Absalom and Achitophel* penned these lines of caution:

> *When ancient buildings nod and threat to fall,*
> *To patch up flaws and buttress up the wall—*
> *Thus far is duty, but here set the mark;*
> *To venture farther is to touch the ark!*
> *To change foundations, cast the frame anew,*
> *Is work for rebels, who base ends pursue.*

INDEX

Page numbers shown in bold face indicate illustrations.

ABBY ALDRICH ROCKEFELLER FOLK ART
   COLLECTION, **97**
Allason, William, 29
Allen-Byrd House, 15, **78**
American Institute of Architects, 44
American Scenic and Historic Preservation
   Society, 44
Anderson, James, House, **81**
   Kitchen, 18, **19**
Apollo Room. *See* Raleigh Tavern
Archaeological Museum, **63**
Archaeology, 40, 48, 49, **50**
Architects, 13, 21, 22, 23, 26
   advisory, 48
   for Colonial Williamsburg, 10, 45, 48, 49
Architecture, 14, 18, 20, 23, 43
   interior, 48
   Virginia, 1, 2, 10, 14, 18
   Williamsburg, 1, 3, 10, 11-23
"Arlington," 39
Association for the Preservation of Vir-
   ginia Antiquities, 43
Athawes, Samuel, 26

"BACON'S CASTLE," 1, 20, **76**
Barber and Wigmaker's Shop, 4, **5**, **90**
Barrel organ, 32
Bartram, John, 39, 40
Bed furniture, 26
Berkeley, Norborne. *See* Botetourt
   Governor [William], 14
"Berkeley," 1
Betty lamps, 34
Beverley, Robert, 26
Bibles, 32
Blacksmiths, 2, 88, **91**
Blair, Archibald, Outbuildings, **85**
   Rev. James, 6, 8
   John, House, 17, **28**, **76**, **77**
   Kitchen, **84**
Blinds, Venetian, **26**, **27**
Bodleian Library, 42, 45
   copperplate, 42, 45, **46**, 49
Books, on architecture, 14, 15, 22, 23, 28
Boot and Shoemaker's shop, **90**
Boston, 3, 10, 43
Botetourt, Norborne Berkeley, Baron de,
   8, 26, 53
   statue of, **92**, **93**
   stove, **27**

Boxwood, **35**, 36, 39, 40, **41**, **81**
Bracken, John, House, **13**, 14
"Brandon," 1
Brick House Tavern, **81**
Bricklayers, 1, 21
Bricks, 1, 14, 16-17, 18, 20, 28, 34, 49, 50
   as ballast, 17
   bond, 16
   making of, **16-17**
   size of, 17
Brown, Fleming, **56**
Bruce, [Philip A.], 14
Brush-Everard House, 25, 26, 40, 60
Bruton Parish Church, **vi**, 3, 8, **9**, 10, 22,
   43, 45, **60**
Bryan House, Garden, 40, **41**, 42
   Kitchen, **84**
Buckland, William, 21
Bucktrout, B., 88
Builders, 1, 18, 20, 21, 22. *See also* Archi-
   tects; Overseers; "Undertakers"
The Builders' Dictionary, 28, 43
Builders' handbooks, 14, 15, 22, 23, 28
Building materials, 1, 14, 15-17, 38. *See*
   also Bricks; Marble; Stone
Burgesses, 6, 9, 10. *See also* Capitol
Burnaby, Andrew, 11
Burying ground, 42
Business area, 94-95
Byrd, William, 28, 34, 80
   House. *See* Allen-Byrd House

CABINETMAKERS, 25, 34, 38, **88**, **89**
   shop, **88**, **89**
Cabins, **18**
Calendar of Virginia State Papers, 31
Campbell, Mrs. Christiana, 81
Candelabra, 34
Candles, 4, 18, 33, 34
Candlesticks, **24**, **30**, **31**, 33, 34, **53**, **58**
Capitals, of Virginia, 3
Capitol, 1, 3, 9, 11, 13, 16, 18, 23, 25, 26,
   29, 43, 45, 49, **67**-70
   act for building, 20
   Bodleian copperplate of, **49**
   Conference Room, **67**
   Council Chamber, 26, 29, 31, 32
   cupola, **20**, **69**
   flag, **69**
   furnishings, 34
   General Court, 20, 26, **68**
   House of Burgesses, 26, 27, **30**, 34, **68**
   rooms in, 25-26, **30**, **31**, **67**, **68**
   wall around, 18

Capitol Landing, 4
Carolina, 8
Carpenters, 1, 20, 21, 27, 88
   tools for, **23**
Carpets, 26, 29
Carter, Robert, 2, 82
Carter, Robert, House, 15, 27, **82**
   Kitchen, **84**
"Carter's Grove," 1, 17
Cary, Henry, 18, 20, 21
Catalpa trees, 52
Cattle, 4
Caulton, Richard, 88
Chairs, 25, 26, 34
Chandeliers, 34, **53**, **54**, **67**, **68**
Charleston, 11
Chimneys, 1, **12**, 13, 15, 16, **18**, **19**, **74**, **75**
China, 34
Chinese influence, 26, 27, **53**, 80
Chowning's Tavern, **ii**, **26**, **27**, **83**
Christ Church, Philadelphia, 43
Churches, 1, 18. *See also* Bruton Parish
   Church
Clocks, 20, 21, **67**
Coaches, 4
Coachmakers, 84, 88, 91
   shop, **91**
Cogar, James L., 48
Coke, John, 80
Coke-Garrett House, **80**
Cole. *See* Taliaferro-Cole Kitchen
Coleman. *See* Waters-Coleman House
Collinson, Peter, 39, 40
Colors, paint. *See* Paint colors
Comedians, company of, 10
Complete Body of Architecture, 14
Continental Congress, 65, 83
Cooking, 33, 34
   utensils, **7**
Coopers' shops, 2
Council, 9, 27, 68. *See also* Capitol, Council
   Chamber
Courthouse of 1770, **63**
Crafts, 4, 6, 88, 89, 90
Craftsmen's tools, **23**, **88**, **89**
Craig, Alexander, House, **22**
Crump, John, House, **47**
Cupolas, **20**, **21**, **69**
Curator, 48
Curtains, bed, **26**, **27**, **58**
   window, **26**, **27**
Custis, John, 39, 40
   Kitchen, 40
   Martha Dandridge, 39
Custis-Maupin Garden, **37**

DADO, 25, 26
Damask, 26, **27**
Dancing, 2, 4
Deane, Elkanah, 82
  House, **82**
  Shop, **91**
Declaration of Independence, 57
Diderot, 27
Dinwiddie, Robert, 10
Doors, 13, 20, 23
Dublin, 84
Duke of Gloucester Street, 6, 11, 13, **36**, 44, 52, **94-95**
Dunmore, John Murray, Earl of, 8, 53, 62
Dyes, 38-39

ENGLAND, 1, 2, 3, 4, 10, 14, 17, 18, 25, 28, 29, 33, 37, 39, 42, 93
Epergne, **33**
Estave, Mr., 6
Evelyn, John, 13, 14
Everard. *See* Brush-Everard House
Evington, Maurice, 23
Exhibition Buildings, 34. *See also* Brush-Everard House; Capitol; Governor's Palace; Magazine and Guardhouse; Public Gaol; Raleigh Tavern; Wythe House

FABRICS, 27
Fairs, 4
Falmouth, 29
Fauquier, Francis, 8
Fences, 36, **38**, **39**, 40, **42**, **86**
Firebacks, 33-34
Fire irons, 32
Fireplaces, 14, 15, 23, **26**, **27**, **28**, 33
Fireworks, 52
Fithian, Philip, 2, 34
Fletcher, S. W., 38
Floor cloths, 26, 29
Floors, 29
Folk art, 97
Franklin, Benjamin, 6
Fredericksburg, 18, 28
Frenchman's Map, 40, **48**
Fruit trees, 37, 40, 42
Furnishings, 4, 24, 25-34, **31**, **33**, 34, 48, 53, 54, 55, **58**, **59**, **60**, **64**, **66**, **67**, **68**

GALT, DR. D. D., 43
  Elizabeth, 43

Gardeners, 40
Gardens, 35-42, **35**, **36**, **37**, **40**
  Bryan, 42
  Custis-Maupin, **37**
  Governor's Palace, 42, 52
  Prentis House, **36**
Garrett. *See* Coke-Garrett House
Gate posts, **39**
Gates, 18, 36
Geddy, James, 4
General Assembly, 21, 32, 36
General Court, 20. *See also* Capitol
Gibbs, James, 23
Gilding, 26
Gilt leather, 26, 27
Glass, window, 27
Glasses, **29**
Glazing, 26
Goldsmiths, 4, 82, 88
Gooch, William, 6
Goodwin, Rev. Dr. W. A. R., 45
Governor's Palace, 1, 3, 4, 8, 13, 14, 15, 21, 23, 25, 29, 45, **46**, 48, **52**, 56, 82
  act to build, 21
  Ballroom, 26, 34, 42
  Bodleian copperplate, **46**
  cupola, **21**
  foundations, **50**
  furnishings, 34, **53**, **54**, **55**
  gardens, 11, 36, 40, 42, 52
  Jefferson's plan for, 22, **45**
  Kitchen, **7**
  lighting, 34
  Little Dining Room, **55**
  mantels, **55**
  Maze and Mount, 42
  outbuildings, **7**, 42, **51**
  Parlor, **54**, 55
  Supper Room, 26, **53**
  Upper Middle Room, 27
  wallpaper in, 26-27
Graham, John M. II, 48
"Green Spring," 14, 42
Greenhow-Repiton House, 47, **72**
Groome, Samuel, 18
Guardhouse, **62**
Guns, 4
Gunsmiths, 88

HA-HA FENCE, **38**
Hairdress, 4
Hairdressers, 88. *See also* Wigmakers
Halfpenny, William, 23

Hallam, Lewis, 9
Ham, recipe for cooking, 34
Hampton Court, 42
Handbooks, for builders, 14, 15, 22, 23, 28
Handel, 8
Hanover Court House, 18
Harpsichords, 32
Harrison, Benjamin, 6
Harvard College, 6, 93
Harwood, Humphrey, 28
Hay's Cabinetmaking Shop, **89**
Hedges, 36, 37, 38, **39**, **40**
Henry, Patrick, 65
Historic American Buildings Survey, 44
History of Fruit Growing in Virginia, 38
History of the First Discovery and Settlement of Virginia, 6
Holly, 37, 39, 42
Hopkins, Alden, 99
Horse races, 4
Horses, 4
House of Burgesses. *See* Burgesses; Capitol
Household utensils, **7**
Houses, Virginia, 1-2, **18**
Houses, Williamsburg, 11, 13, 14, 15, 16, 28, 32
  Allen-Byrd House, 15, **78**
  Anderson, James, House, 19, **81**
  Blair, John, House, 17, **28**, **76**, 77
  Bracken, John, House, 13, 14
  Brick House Tavern. *See* Brick House Tavern
  Brush-Everard House, 25, 40, **56**
  Bryan House, 40
  Capitol. *See* Capitol
  Chowning's Tavern. *See* Chowning's Tavern
  Coke-Garrett House, **80**
  Craig, Alexander, House, **22**
  Deane, Elkanah, House, **82**
  Geddy, James, House, **61**
  Governor's Palace. *See* Governor's Palace
  Greenhow-Repiton House, 47, **72**
  Guardhouse, **62**
  Jail. *See* Public Gaol
  Jones, Orlando, House, **76**
  Lightfoot House, 14, **74**
  Magazine. *See* Magazine
  Market Square Tavern. *See* Market Square Tavern
  Moody House, 74, **75**
  Orrell House, 14, **74**
  Plans of, 13, 14, 15, 21
  President's House, 15, **92**, 93

Houses, Williamsburg—*Continued*
　Public Records Office. *See* Public Records Office
　Quarter, **15**
　Raleigh Tavern. *See* Raleigh Tavern
　Randolph, Peyton, House, 25, **26**, 27, **28**, 83
　Robert Carter House, 15, 27, **82**
　Scrivener House, **47**
　Semple House, **80**
　Stith, Mary, Forge, **78**
　Tayloe, John, House, 14, **74**
　Theater. *See* Theaters
　Travis House, 74, **75**
　Tucker, St. George, House, 12, **79**
　Waters-Coleman House, 74, **75**
　Wren Building, 1, 3, **8**, **92**, **93**, 94
　Wythe House, 15, **26**, 27, **28**, 33, 34, 40, **57**, **58**, **59**
　　Outbuildings, **79**
　See also Kitchens; Shops
Huntington Library, 48
Hurricane shade, **34**

INDEPENDENCE, DECLARATION OF, 57
Independence Hall, 43
India, 38
Indians, 1, 3, 93
Information Center, **96**
Inkwells, **30**, 32
Insurance policies, 44
Ireland, 33, 91
Italy, 33

JACQUELIN, MARTHA, 29
Jail. *See* Public Gaol
James River, 1, 2, 13
Jamestown, 1, 3, 11, 13, 14
Jefferson, Thomas, 6, 8, 16, 21, 22, 23, 57, 65
　plans by, 22, **45**, 48
Jefferson, Thomas, Foundation, 44
Jeffriess, 25
Jewelry, 4
Jones, Hugh, 8, 13
　Orlando, House, **76**

KENDALL, JOSHUA, 27
Kendrew, A. E., 45
Kidd, Joseph, 26
Kimball, Fiske, 11, 44
Kings and Queens (game), **53**
Kitchen utensils, **7**, 33

Kitchens, 33, 40, 42, **84**
　Anderson, James, Kitchen, **19**
　Blair, John, Kitchen, **84**
　Bryan Kitchen, **84**
　Custis Kitchen, 40
　Governor's Palace Kitchen, **7**
　Ludwell-Paradise Kitchen, **84**
　Robert Carter Kitchen, **84**
　Taliaferro-Cole Kitchen, **84**
　Tucker, St. George, Kitchen, **12**
Knight, Madame, 16

LAFAYETTE, GENERAL, 83
Landscape architects, 45
Langley, Batty, 23
Lanterns, **66**
Leather, gilt, 26, 27
Lee, Robert E., 3, 44
Lee, Robert E., Memorial Foundation, 44
Leedstown, 25
Levingston, William, 9
Lexington, Battle of, 62
Libraries, 23
Lightfoot House, 14, **74**
Lighting, 34. *See also* Candelabra; Candles; Candlesticks; Chandeliers; Lanterns
London, 4, 6, 9, 11, 13, 18, 22, 25, 29, 39, 55, 88
London *Post Boy*, 8
Looking glasses, 32
Lots, Williamsburg, 11, 13, 36
Ludwell-Paradise Coach House, **85**
　Kitchen, **84**

MADISON, JAMES, **31**
Magazine, 44, **62**
Mantelpieces, **26**, 27, **28**, **55**
Maps, 40, 42, 44, **48**
Marble, 28
Marbleized wood, 32
Market Square Tavern, **26**, **27**
Marl, 28, 49
Marshall, John, 6
Maryland, 8, 39
Mason, George, 65
Massachusetts Historical Society, 48
Mazes, 42
The Merchant of Venice, 9, **10**
Methodists, 9
Middle Plantation, 1, 3, 9, 11, 18
Middlesex County, 18
Mills, 1
　paper, 6
Minetree, David, 18

Minor, Dabney, 31
Monroe, James, 6
"Monticello," 44
Moody House, 74, **75**
Moorehead, S. P., 45
Morris, James, 18
　Robert, 23
"Mount Vernon," 43
Mount Vernon Ladies' Association, 43
Mulberry trees, 4, 6, 37-38
Murray, John. *See* Dunmore
Music, 3, 8, 32

NASH, MRS. SUSAN H., 48
National Trust for Historic Preservation, 44
National Park Service, 44
New England, 14
New Kent County, 17, 18
New York, 3, 16, 33
Newspapers. *See Virginia Gazette*
Nicholson, Francis, 11, 13, 38, 86
"Nomini Hall," 2, 34, 82
Norfolk, 48
North Carolina, 39, 40
Norton, John, & Sons, 29

OGLE, CUTHBERT, 8
Orrell House, 14, **74**
Outbuildings, 17
　Plantation, 1, 2
　Williamsburg, **12**, **19**, 35-36, 40, 42, 51, **84**, **85**
Overseers, 20, 21
Oxford, 42, 45

PAIN, WILLIAM, 23
Paint colors, 14, 26, 29, 31, 32, 72
Painting of houses, 29-32
Paintings, 33
Palace. *See* Governor's Palace
Palace Green, 9, 13, 82
Paper mill, 6
Parks, William, 6
Parliament, 10, 17
Pennsylvania, 8, 39
Pens, quill, **30**, 32
Perry, Shaw and Hepburn, 45
Philadelphia, 3, 11, 39, 43
Pictures, 32, 33
Pillory, **70**
Plans, for houses, **13**, **14**, **15**, 21
Plantations, houses on, 1-2, 18
Plants, 36-38, 39, 40
Playhouses, 9, 10

Plays, 9, 10
Poems by a Gentleman of Virginia, 6
The Poor Planter's Physician, 6
Portland stone, 28
Portrait painters, 33
Powder magazines, 18. *See also* Magazine
Powell, Benjamin, vi
Pratt, Matthew, 33
Prentis House, 36
    Store, 46
The Present State of Virginia, 13
President's House, 15, **92**, 93
Primatt, Stephen, 35
Princess Anne County, 16
Printing office, 6
Printers, 6
Prints, copperplate, 25
Privies, 40
Public Gaol, **70, 71**
Public Records Office, 16, **17**
"Publick Times," 3-4
Purbeck stone, 28, 29, 50

QUARTER, **15**
"Quickset" hedges, **39**
Quill pens, 30, 32

RALEIGH TAVERN, 34, **65**
    Apollo Room, 46
    Dining Room, **24**
    furnishings, 34
    stairway, **66**
    Taproom, **64**
Randolph, Mrs. Betty, 28
    Edmund, 6
    Sir John, 39
    Peyton, 28, 65, 83
        House, 25, **26**, 27, **28**, 83
Repiton. *See* Greenhow-Repiton House
Research Department, 48
Restoration, principles of, 48-50
Rhinoceros, The Sign of the, **90**
Richmond, 3, 31
Robertson's Windmill, **87**
Rochambeau, General, 83
Rockefeller, John D., Jr., 45
Rolfe, John, 1
Roofs, 13, 14, 20, 23, **65**, 72
"Rosewell," 14
Rugs, 29

SADDLES, 4
St. Luke's Church, 1
St. Peter's Church, 17, 18

Sautier Plans, 40, 42
Schuylkill, 39
Scrivener House, **47**
Semple House, **80**
Shaw, Thomas Mott, **16**
Shingles, 14, 72
"Shirley," 1, 14
Shoemaker's Shop, **90**
Shoes, 4
Shops, Williamsburg, 4, **5**, **83**, **89**, **90**, **91**, 94-95
    Barber and Wigmaker's Shop, 4, 5, **90**
    Blacksmith's Shop, **91**
    Boot and Shoemaker's Shop, **90**
    Cabinetmaker's Shop, **89**
    Deane Shop, 91
    Robertson's Windmill, **87**
    Shoemaker's Shop, **90**
    Wigmaker's Shop, 4, 5, **90**
Shrubs, 36-38, 39, 40, 42
Shurcliff, Arthur A., 45
Shutters, 27
Silk industry, 6
Smith, John, 32, 38
Smithfield, 1
Snuff boxes, 32
Society for the Advancement of Useful Knowledge, 8
Speaker's chair, 34
Spinets, 32
Spotswood, Alexander, 9, **21**, 52
Stairways, 15, **66, 80**
Stamp Act, 4
Steeples, 22
Stith, Mary, Shop, **73**
    Tin Shop, **78**
    William, 6, 32
Stocks, 70
Stone, imported, 28
Stoves, 27
    Botetourt, **27**
"Stratford," 1, 3, 44
Stuart, Gilbert, 31
Surry County, 1
Swan, Abraham, 23

TABLES, 25
Taliaferro, Richard, 21, 57
Taliaferro-Cole Kitchen, **84**, 86
Tayloe, John, House, 14, **74**
Theaters, 8, 9, 10, 76, 77
Thoreau, 25
Tobacco, 1, 2
Todd House, 18

Tools, carpenters', **23**
    craftsmen's, **88, 89**
Trades, in Williamsburg, 4, 6. *See also* Crafts; Shops
The Tragedy of Cato, 9
Travis House, 74, **75**
Trees, 36-38, 39, 40, 42, 49, 52
"Tuckahoe," 1
Tucker, St. George, 79
    House, **79**
    Kitchen, **12**
Tyler, John, 6
Typographia, 6

UNDERTAKERS (BUILDERS), **22**
Upholsterers, 26, 88

VENETIAN blinds, 26, 27
Virginia. *See* Architecture, Virginia; Houses; Plantations
Virginia Gazette, 4, 6, 9, 22, 23, 26, 27, 33, 50, 88, 93
Vitruvius, 23
Vobe, Mrs., 33

WAINSCOTING, 25, 26, 32
Walks, garden, 36, 40, 42
Wallpaper, **26**, 27
Wall treatment, 25-27
Walls, surrounding, 18, 36
Walter, Thomas Ustick, 43
Ware, Isaac, 14, 23
Warner's Almanack, 32
Washington, George, 9, 10, 39, 65, 81
    John Augustine, 43
    Martha, 39
Washington, D.C., 43
Waters-Coleman House, 74, **75**
Webb, Philip, 49
West, Mr., 33
Westmoreland County, 2, 44
"Westover," 1, 14, 34
Wetherburn's Tavern, 66
Wheelwrights, 91
Whitewash, 31
Whitefield, Rev. George, **9**
The Whole Body of the Laws of Virginia, 6
Wigmaker, **5**
    shop of, 4, **5**, **90**
William III, 3
William and Mary College, 1, 3, 6, 8, 9, 11, 13, 29, 45, 48, 81, **92, 93**
    Jefferson's plan for, 22
    President's House, 15, **92**
    Wren Building, 1, 3, **8**, 22, 48, **92, 93**, 94

Williamsburg, 1, 3, 4, 6, 8, 11
  act directing building, 11
  architecture in, 3, 10, 11-23. *See also*
    Houses, Williamsburg
  business district, 94-95
  drawing of, **44**
  gardens in, 35-42, 45
  houses in. *See* Houses, Williamsburg
  lots in, 11, 13, 36
  manufactures in, 4
  population, 3
  "Publick Times," 3-4

Williamsburg—*Continued*
  restoration of, 43-95
  shopping district, 94-95
  shops of. *See* Shops
  streets, 6, 11, 13, 36, **44**, 52, **94**
  theaters, 8, 9, 10, 76
  trades in, 4, 6. *See also* Crafts; Shops
Window curtains, 26
Windows, 13, 20, 22, 23, 49, 50
  casement, 27
  sash, 27
Windmill, Robertson's, **87**

Wren, Sir Christopher, 8, 13
Wren Building. *See* William and Mary
  College
Wythe, George, 6, 23, 34, 57, 65
  House, **15**, **26**, 27, **28**, **33**, 34. **35**, 40, **57**,
    58, **59**
  Outbuildings, **85**

Yew, 37, 39, 40
York County, 81, 88
York River, 1, 13, 29

CREDITS FOR ILLUSTRATIONS

The photographs in the book, in large part made expressly for it, are with a few exceptions the work of four cameramen, Herbert Matter, Thomas Williams, Richard Garrison, and John Crane. Mr. Matter took his shots in mid-winter and as the buds began to open in the springtime. Mr. Williams was tireless in his efforts to furnish for the book photographs necessary to the illustration of the text or depicting unusual aspects of the Williamsburg scene. Mr. Garrison's and Mr. Crane's pictures were taken from time to time during the last few years. Additional photographs of unusual merit are the work of Robert C. Lautman and Steve Toth.

The following abbreviations have been used in identifying the photographs and drawings listed in the credit index below: M—Herbert Matter; W—Thomas Williams; G—Richard Garrison; C—John Crane; R.L.—Robert C. Lautman; T—Steve Toth; C.W.—Colonial Williamsburg Files; L—Left; R—Right. Drawings not otherwise identified are by the authors.

Front end paper, Keys—W; door detail—M; **Frontispiece**—M; v—W; vi—W; 2—Bryant and Gay, *A Popular History of the United States;* 3—W; 4—L. Paul Lacroix, *Eighteenth Century, Its Institutions, Customs, and Costumes: France 1700-1789;* 5—M; 7—T; 8—W; 9, L—W; R—A. S. Turberville, *English Men and Manners in the Eighteenth Century;* 10, Planter—E. R. Billings, *Tobacco, Its History, Varieties, Culture, Manufacture and Use;* 12—W; 13—C.W.; 15—C; 16—Drawings by Thomas Mott Shaw; Photograph—M; 17—T; 18, L—Harvard University Collection; R—Historic American Buildings Survey; 19—M; 20—W; 21—W; 22—C; 23—W; 24—C; 25—C.W.; 26, No. 1—T; No. 2—Diderot, *Encyclopedia;* No. 3—W; No. 4—C.W.; No. 5—T; Wallpaper—T; 27, Damask—Courtesy, Curator; No. 6—M; 28, No. 1—T; No. 2—M; No. 3—W; 29, Glassware—C.W.; 30—T; 31—T;

32, Marbleized woodwork—W; Flask—C.W.; 33, L—C.W.; R—T; 34—C.W.; 35—W; 37—C; 39—W; 40—M; 41—C; 42—T; 44—Courtesy, the Century Company; 45—Courtesy, Massachusetts Historical Society; 46, Palace—W; Palace drawing—Courtesy, Bodleian Library; Raleigh Interior—C.W.; Raleigh interior drawing—Benson J. Lossing, *The Pictorial Field-book of the Revolution;* Wigmaker's Shop, L—G; Wigmaker's Shop, R—C.W.; 47, John Crump House, L—C.W., R—W; Greenhow-Repiton House water color—Artist unknown; Greenhow-Repiton House—C; Scrivener House, L—C.W.; Scrivener House, R—C; 48, Frenchman's Map—Courtesy, College of William and Mary; 49—Courtesy, Bodleian Library; 50, Plan—Division of Architecture of C.W.; Photographs—C.W.; 51—M; 52, above—T; other photographs—W; 53, above—C; below—M; 54—M; 55, above—C; below—M; 56—C; 57—W; 58, above—T; below—M; 59, above—C.W.; below—T; 60—W; 61, above—T; below—C.W.; 62—W; 63, above—W; below, L—Cook Collection; below, R—C.W.; 64—C.W.; 65, above—M; below—C; 66—T; 67, above—W; below—T; 68, above—M; below—W; 69—M; 70, above—M; below—W; 71—M; 72—W; 73—T; 74, above—T; below, L—C; below, R—W; 75, above—M; below—W; 76, above—G; below—T; 77—T; 78, above—M; below—C.W.; 79—M; 80, above—W; below, L—Authors; below, R—C.W.; 81, L—W; R—G; 82, above—G; below—C; 83, above—T; below—W; 84, above, R—G; other photographs—W; 85, above—M; below—W; 86—M; 87—C.W.; 88—M; 89, above—T; below—W; 90, above, L—C; above, R—W; below, L—W; below, R—W; 91, above—W; below—M; 92, No. 1—M; No. 2—C.W.; Nos. 3 and 4—W; 93, above—M; below—W; 94, above—T; 95—Drawing by Vernon Wooten; 96, above—C.W.; below—C.W.; 97, above—C.W.; below—R.L.